Th Compass Club

Club

Directing the Arrow Toward Peace

Jackie O'Connor

Scripture quotations and references are adapted from the Revised Standard Version of the Bible, copyright 1946, 1952, 1971, and the New Revised Standard Version of the Bible, 1989 by the Division of Christian Education of the National Council of the Churches of Christ in the United States of America and are used with permission.

Other Biblical References used include:

-*The Holy Bible Catholic Journaling Bible: The New American Bible*, 2017 Our Sunday Visitor Publishing Division

-*Catechism of the Catholic Church*, 1995 an Image Book, Published by Doubleday

-*United States Catholic Catechism for Adults*, 2011, Published by the United States Council of Catholic Bishops

-*Prove It! The Catholic Teen Bible NAB, Revised Edition* 2011 by Our Sunday Visitor

Cover Design: Grayson Hartwick
Photography: Grayson Hartwick
Scripture Photo Images: Kelly O'Connor
Compass, Bible & Arrow Illustrations: Jessica Sack

Paperback ISBN-13: 978-1-6628-2277-3   Ebook ISBN-13: 978-1-6628-2278-0

Xulon Press
2301 Lucien Way #415
Maitland, FL 32751
407.339.4217
www.xulonpress.com

For more information:
https://www.thecompassclub.org

Brothers and Sisters:

I, a prisoner for the Lord, urge you to live in a manner worthy of the call you have received, with all the humility and gentleness, with patience, bearing with one another through love, and striving to preserve the unity of the Spirit through the *bond of peace:*

One body and one Spirit, as you were also called to the one hope of your call; one Lord, one faith, one baptism, one God and Father of all, who is over all, through all, and in all.

But grace was given to each of us according to the measure of Christ's gift.

And he gave some as apostles, others as prophets, others as evangelists, others as pastors and teachers, to equip the holy ones for the work of ministry, for building up the Body of Christ, until we attain a unity of faith and knowledge of the Son of God, to mature manhood to the extent of the full stature of Christ.

-St. Paul's Letter to the Ephesians
Ephesians 4:1-7, 11-13

TABLE OF CONTENTS

John 15:16

"You did not choose me, but I chose you and appointed you that you should go and bear fruit and that your fruit should abide, so that whatever you ask the Father in my name, He may give it to you."

Dedication – 5

Author's Note - 6

Acknowledgments - 11

Reader's Guide - 12

1. *The Core of the Compass is Christ* - 15

2. *Others: The Relationships You Choose* - 29

3. *The Moral Compass: Modesty and Morality* - 43

4. *Prayer Power: First Things First* - 62

5. *Almsgiving and Adoration: It Is in Giving That We Receive* - 83

6. *Scripture: The Soul Strengthening Tool* - 103

7. *Sacraments and Saints: Soul Food and Guides for the Journey* - 117

Compass Club Appendix and Prayer Resources - 144
National Retreats/Bible Studies/Social Media - 156
Compass Club Book Shelf - 158
Christian-Catholic Gifts - 162
Compass Club Music Playlist - 163

DEDICATION

This book is dedicated to God, my heavenly Father, who nudged me for seven years to get this book published. I share this dedication with my daughter, Kelly, who insisted that what I felt called to write needed to be shared with her generation and the caregivers guiding them.

She pushed me along when I lacked confidence in my ability to write it. During many car rides to and from school, she shared the life challenges she was facing, first in middle school, and later through high school. She believed that this spiritual life guide could help families to live more peacefully with greater hope, grow deeper in their faith, and strengthen their relationship with God.

Lastly, I was blessed to have Father Ed Hamilton, who was my spiritual advisor for seven years and also felt this would be a great resource for today's families. Before he died in 2018, he reassured me that the Holy Spirit would guide me. He was right.

AUTHOR'S NOTE

An image of God holding me in the palm of His hand came to my mind one day in the image of a *compass*. He was my Creator, but I ultimately still had full control of my life direction and He would protect and guide me as long as I kept Him at the core of my inner being.

The *arrow of my soul* would be strengthened by His grace and directed toward *His will* for my life based on how much I actively chose to remain in a relationship with Him. *It seemed like a great metaphor for a more peaceful life.* At that moment, I felt divinely inspired to write these thoughts down. That was seven years ago.

It occurred to me then that every single day, all of us are in this *same position* of having this power and divinely inspired opportunities that are best for living out our true mission in life, but we sometimes make things more difficult than they need to be.

We stray from His heart and rely on our instincts and the opinions of others. We don't stay close to Him. *The disposition of our soul and core of our being is vulnerable.* This is why many of us lack a sense of true peace and tranquility that God intended for us when He created us in His image and likeness.

The purpose of a compass is to give direction from where you are and to help you navigate where you desire to go. At the center of the compass, there is an arrow that is directed by *movement and activity* based on a gravitational pull to several quadrants: north, south, east, and west. Whoever is holding the compass, directs the arrow.

In this book, the compass is a symbol that represents our life and the arrow is the mechanism by which we *direct our soul* from the center of the compass. Today, many of us feel pulled in so many directions and we do not have peace in our minds and hearts. We are oftentimes stressed, tired, and confused about how to find balance with the many stimuli and choices presented to us.

We lack confidence and hope in a future that is unknown. The expectation to manage everything well affects us physically, emotionally, and spiritually. That conflict of energies greatly impacts our well-being, family life, and important relationships.

The Compass Club is a practical Catholic-Christian spiritual life guide where the image of a compass is used to represent and illustrate *us in relationship to God and the world* around us. You will be given strategies you can use to *strengthen your soul* and consistently direct the arrow to only *those areas of focus* that truly empower you to live your best life each day in more positive ways.

This life guide has supported me throughout many painful and challenging life experiences. It has become a way to consistently have peace in my heart and soul no matter what obstacles come my way.

Strategies presented here have kept me grounded in God's truth when relationships are difficult, worldly influences threaten to rob the sanctity of my home, and past childhood wounds surface that force me to manage feelings that I've suppressed from myself and hidden from those that love me.

I've learned first-hand that the only way to stay hopeful and trusting no matter how much chaos surrounds me is to *make better life choices using these strategies*. When I consistently focus on the path leading toward God, *I feel extraordinary peace.*

I've identified seven areas that always direct me back to my core and keep me grounded in faith. I've offered these suggestions because I have continued to enjoy a path to peace by focusing only on those areas that *most directly* strengthen my soul. I have found a path to life-sustaining peace that lasts.

This life guide works.

I believe this guide will empower you and your families to live with less discouragement, depression, stress, and anxiety in your daily decision-making.

You will always have a way back to a peace-filled core foundation when you feel lost and disillusioned by the negative and compromising worldly influences around you. Consider this *Compass Club* model as a way to connect you to others in more meaningful relationships and most importantly, foster a deeper connection to God.

We go through our days losing that connection, feeling out of control, and being led to areas that are not ultimately good for us mentally, physically, or spiritually. This chaotic life harms us as individuals and does not create opportunities for *authentic* connections in our family relationships.

We are not living life to our fullest potential. We are depleted of positive energy by just trying to keep up with the world's expectations of us.

If you are a parent, guardian, teacher, or caretaker, I also hope this book will help you to better guide those entrusted to your care and well-being. Your children will also be inspired to make better life choices and feel more confident and in control of their actions and behaviors.

So many parents today worry about the future lives of their children and the choices they are making in a socially challenging world. We worry if they will be safe from harm. There are so many temptations our children face at any given moment and we hope and pray they choose wisely. It's exhausting to worry so much. This is not a healthy lifestyle for us emotionally nor physically.

I have been mentally strengthened in every quadrant of my life by adopting this *Compass Club* life guide. I do not worry like I used to. I feel such unshakeable inner peace. The tranquility I feel has directly impacted all of my relationships in so many positive ways that I simply had to find a way to share these ideas.

For years, I felt called to share these ideas and strategies with others, but I lacked confidence that I should be the one to write this. I'm not a theologian nor do I have an advanced degree in religion or psychology.

I'm am an ordinary soul.

God asked me to simply trust Him during my quiet moments of prayer and give Him my, "yes." He continued to remind me that His greatest desire is for us to have an intimate friendship with Him and to feel His peace. Above all, to experience the most abundant and life-sustaining peace in our earthly lives, we must stay on the path leading toward Him.

The Compass Club model will offer structure and accountability for *intentional living goals* that lead to a peace that is sustaining. Most importantly, these strategies will support you no matter what challenging life circumstances come your way.

There's no such thing as a perfect life devoid of pain and hardship but knowing ways to remain spiritually centered and hopeful while carrying our crosses is invaluable.

God created us as members of the Body of Christ with His intention for us to experience an abundance of peace *in communion* with each other. His grace was given to us in Baptism to make that peace possible.

Many of these ideas are presented in the Catholic faith's traditions, but any Christian who deeply desires inner peace will benefit from these suggestions.

We are all children of the same God.

Imagine a world where everyone belongs to the same *Compass Club*; a united spiritual community where life focus is *directed to only those areas* that yield the most abundant peace that God has promised to us.

We will then become more strongly engaged members of the Body of Christ and be the eyes, ears, feet, and hands of Christ to do His greatest work on Earth.

We will be inspired every day to confidently be our most authentic selves with the strongest soul possible. We will feel the intimate power within us to direct our soul toward a path to peace that always *keeps Christ as the core of our lives.*

The Compass Club can become something we choose to *join in our hearts for the benefit of our souls* and consequently, we can share that joy and peace with others.

ACKNOWLEDGMENTS

I'd like to thank my beloved husband, Jerry, for giving me the time to invest in preparing this work. If not for his hard work, devotion, and support of our family, I'd be working full-time and would not have had the time to write this.

I'd also like to thank my amazing sisters in Christ who prayed for me, provided feedback, and inspired me by their faithful lives over the years as I was writing: Tanya Braithwaite, Ginny Bullock, Marlene Burke, Theresa Callaghan, Lisa Corcoran, Dotsie Cuillo, Julie Curtin, Jen Devine, Michelle Haley, Honor Jones, Katie Keating, Lisa Kopertowski, Peggy Kravitz, Lizanne Pando, Patricia Smith, Maryalice Snarponis, Michele Walton, and Mary Zsembik.

Some great men have been equally impactful as spiritual mentors: Joe Aquilante, John Braithwaite, Father Allan Fitzgerald, Mark Griswold, Marty Kenney, Eddie Morris, Tony Mullen (deceased), Jim Ryan, Gerald O'Connor Sr., Father Scott Reilly, Pat Welde, and Father Charles Zlock who are men with strong faith convictions. Their daily witness reaffirmed for me that that this book needed to support priests, grandfathers, fathers, sons, uncles, brothers, and male educators.

I was able to author this book because these men and women have truly inspired me in the way they passionately live their faith in their thoughts, words, and actions.

They exude peace in their lives.

In many ways, they were honorary first members of the *Compass Club*, supporting the direction of the *arrow of my soul*.

READER'S GUIDE

In the next seven chapters, you are going to explore seven quadrants of the compass that will guide your decisions toward your most *peaceful* life. The word compass is used as an acronym for each chapter: C.O.M.P.A.S.S to help the reader remember the quadrants most easily.

This book is structured to be flexible with chapters that can be used in the following learning environments:

- Independent reading/self-study
- Church Bible study
- Sacramental prep supplement
- Parish retreat
- Lenten preparation guide
- Book Club
- Family program-homeschooling

Scripture is abundantly and intentionally placed throughout the book as chapter-opening passages, end of chapter exercises, and supplemental studies in the index. These are included to inspire intimate reflection and offer real-world connections toward changes in behavior. The Bible, as the living Word of God, is as relevant today as it was thousands of years ago. Be sure to underline those passages that speak to your soul.

An ancient Catholic prayer process called "Lectio Divina" is recommended as a guide for reading scripture throughout this book. This ancient practice offers life instruction for the soul with God's Word through the intercession of the Holy Spirit that opens up so many intimate opportunities to truly encounter God.

There are four simple steps to this process:

1. *Reading* the passage simply for the literal meaning. (Lectio)

2. *Mediating* on the meaning and thinking about how this speaks to your life by placing yourself in the passage. (Meditation)

3. *Praying* about the scripture and asking God conversationally what His intention might be for your life. (Prayer)

4. *Contemplation* on God's Word should lead to some degree of transformation of heart by complete trust and openness to His grace and conversion. (Contemplatio) [1]

End-of-Chapter Materials:

- **Chapter Opening Scripture Passages:** These verses represent the overall theme and focus of each chapter.

- **Compass Connections:** Scripture verses that stimulate meditative reflections that will drive the transformation of heart, mind, and soul.

- **Compass Commitment:** A place to identify and list new goals for lifestyle changes.

- **Directing the Arrow:** Ideas for engaging in *action-driven* activities for the soul.

- **Journal Exercises:** Thoughts that come to mind as you read are to be placed here. Do not wait to get to the end of a chapter.

- **Lectio Divina Supplemental Passages:** pages 3 and 139 include longer scriptural passages for deeper reflection.

- **Supplemental Scripture Study:** pages 142 and 143 include seventeen scripture passages for further study.

You can read this book without doing any of the end-of-chapter reflections and exercises, but the goal of experiencing lasting peace is more possible when making time for prayer and scripture reflections.

The index includes the works of gifted authors who have spiritually fed my soul for years. The list is a beginning, but certainly not all-inclusive. These resources support accountability and provide ideas for a busy lifestyle.

Spiritual content that is reviewed regularly will empower you to live your faith with intelligence, courage and conviction. A lifestyle of eating nutritious food is healing for the body; *scripture helps to nourish and strengthen the soul.*

The index includes the following:

- Catholic-Christian Websites
- Catholic Prayers
- National Retreats/Bible Studies/Social Media
- Smartphone Resources
- Compass Club Christian-Catholic Gifts
- Compass Club Book Shelf
- Compass Club Spotify Music Playlist

THE GOLDEN ARROW

The Golden Arrow represented throughout the book is a symbol that was given to St. Mary of Peter, a Carmelite nun who experienced many visions of Jesus in the 1840's. At that time, atheism and blasphemy (the poisoned arrows) against the Holy Face and Name of Jesus were as common as they are today. She was asked to spread the "Golden Arrow Prayer", as a means of restoring peace in the world and the conversion of sinners. The three rings symbolize the Holy Trinity. This powerful prayer can be found in the index.

CHAPTER 1:

THE CORE OF THE COMPASS IS CHRIST

Psalm 139

"O Lord, you have probed me, and you know me;
you know when I sit and when I stand;
you understand my thoughts from afar.
My journeys and my rest you scrutinize,
with all my ways you are familiar.

Truly you have formed my inmost being;
you knit me in my mother's womb.
I give you thanks that I am fearfully,
wonderfully made;
wonderful are your works.

Probe me, O God, and know my heart;
try me, and know my thoughts;
See if my way is crooked,
and lead me in the way of old."

The fitness industry, in the last ten years, has strongly promoted that using your core for movements is the way to be physically stronger and more balanced. Many fitness classes today remind the participants to strengthen their core and remain strong from that position because it *minimizes injury* and will empower them with a much stronger sense of well-being. We are reminded to *engage our core* with every exercise we do.

What if we applied this mindset as a life exercise, relating instead to our *soul* by choosing Christ as our *core* foundation? What if He were truly the center of everything we do?

We spend thousands of dollars each year to improve our physical bodies, yet our internal self and the spiritual core of our souls are often left neglected. Perhaps becoming *fit instruments of God's grace* is a fitness goal that has the power to deliver the peace we seek?

Many today enjoy varying stress-relieving activities like yoga, meditation, and mindfulness classes, but if our internal sensor, our soul, is conflicted, we will still feel off balance. Exercising the physical body has immeasurable benefits, but if we are not doing the same for our souls, we will not have inner peace.

On page three, we read St. Paul's Letter to the Ephesians 4:1-7, 11-13 that was written over 2,000 years ago when he urged the people to strive for a *bond of peace*, and they would enjoy if they lived in a manner worthy of their call.

Like the Ephesians, we are also being drawn away from a spirit of unity, peace, and love that would allow us to build up the kingdom of God here on Earth and experience the full extent of God's grace to follow our *calling*.

We face even greater challenges and social pressures today that our more modern world creates. No matter how much we focus on physical fitness, many of us still need emotional healing. We can't find our calling and know our purpose if our souls are left unattended.

Social media is one significant influence that has robbed us of the time our souls need to find this balance. It has become an overwhelming and constant stimulus. We know we are spending too much time with it, but we can't find a way to resist using it. Much of the content brings toxic energy and stresses that truly impact our emotional health in negative ways.

Our society has become obsessed with information that is shared and *valued* in relationships with strangers, yet we are pulled into this activity daily. Time invested here has changed the way we view ourselves and our relationships with each other. We allow others to influence our opinions and direct our decisions because our *centeredness* comes from too many external influences.

Technology use and social media access can offer many positive benefits and yet, when it comes to human interaction, it can negatively affect our self-esteem and pull us away from the core of our true identities as children of God, the Father, and our Divine Creator.

Escalating rates of suicide, depression, drug use, eating disorders, and domestic violence today validate the harsh reality that there are far too many of us who lack the coping mechanisms to deal with these pressures. Our children have become the most vulnerable population.

Adults also feel this loss of healthy, soulful connectivity. The vast majority of us do not love ourselves as God intended. *The core of our soul is not being fed by choices that strengthen us.* Could there be another alternative to living healthier lives that is more positively constructive to support our daily choices?

I attended Mass a few years ago when the pastor was overwhelmed by the standing room only attendance at his healing service. Visitors from parishes all over the state had come to see a Catholic layperson from the Philippines who had the reputation for bringing about miraculous healing through the intercession of the Blessed Mother, holy oil, and the use of roses.

The pastor spoke passionately from the pulpit saying, "We have doctors for each body part, but why don't you come to church regularly to see the Divine Healer? Every Sunday should look like this but sadly, the pews are empty."

The large masses of people had come to witness a miracle, but they failed to recall that healing opportunities were already available to their souls during any regular Mass celebration.

When God formed us, He intended for us to live beyond our expectations of ourselves. He hoped that we would stay truly connected to Him, so we could more fully embrace the gifts that He desired to give us and bear the most abundant fruit possible.

He created us for greatness far beyond what we think we can do alone. He wanted us to be formed into saints who would return to Him after using our gifts to make the world better. He promised us the grace to get the job done well, yet we neglect to use this grace, or have we simply lost our way and forgotten how to access it?

Many of us have yet to realize our full potential because we are still allowing the world to direct our thoughts, words, and actions. We dedicate more of our time to physical fitness because we want to look attractive and feel better physically, but even when we accomplish those fitness goals, we can still feel disillusioned and unsatisfied. Placing a higher priority on the health of our souls is a foundational principle of the *Compass Club* mentality.

At the very *core* of our compass is our innermost being, our soul, which needs Christ inside it. The strength of our soul or our *conscience* and the direction of the arrow of our Compass is dependent on embracing the truths of *who* created us, *why* we are here on this earth, and *what* we came to do in this world. When we embrace God as our Divine Creator, we know that He greatly desires to live in us and to share an intimate friendship with Him. Above all, we are part of a bigger community as treasured members of the Body of Christ.

This knowledge *alone* should comfort us and give us such confidence and peace, yet we forget this divine truth because we are being pulled every day by too many forces outside of ourselves that are not healthy or steadying our direction toward tranquil living.

The quality of the air around us and the gravitational pull of a multitude of influences will direct the compass that we control, and we move in the direction of our *intention*. That movement is guided by our conscience, free will, and how strong our relationship is with our God.

We can only live this way by remaining connected to the Him by seeking that heavenly power that guides and directs our actions daily. Many ordinary saints that lived before us accomplished extraordinary things because they lived virtuous lives with Christ as the core of their souls.

When we fly on an airplane, we are instructed that in the event of an emergency landing, we should put on our oxygen masks first before placing the masks on our children. That same idea applies here. We can't expect to have peace and life balance with a strong physical core unless our spiritual core is likewise engaged. Our children and all those who rely on us for advice, guidance, and encouragement will be best served when we are steady and ready.

We were not created to be solitary human beings. We were divinely created to be *in communion* with each other. In fact, this gravitational pull to be actively part of a very social world is perfectly normal and healthy *if* we are choosing wisely. This is why social media has become so addictive.

Social media outlets offer an incessant activity that gives us thousands of virtual connections, but much of that is anything but healthy. There's an intensity to this engagement and a pull to interact that is very time-consuming. Families, friends, and even strangers are engaging with us and our children virtually on a constant basis. Sometimes we can forget when we've had an actual in-person conversation rather than one that was online.

This longing to connect and belong does not necessarily feed our souls positively and can be emotionally harmful and very stressful over time. We are connecting more often than not to people, places, and things that are not always the healthiest choices.

We know this fact, yet we still are pulled in by temptations we find hard to manage. Some of us even put limits on our phones and computers, so we can set reasonable time allotments for social media activity.

We know this addictive behavior is out of control. The problem with this magnetic attraction is that it leads to an increasing loss of identity and our *authentic selves*. Our validation is coming from others who may not even know us or care what is best for us.

If we can instead engage in more activities that reinforce that *Christ is our core and our soul is a priority;* we will be less likely to need the validation from these social media outlets. We are likely to become less attracted to it because Christ's peace will be enough. Fear of missing out would no longer be an issue for us.

Today's society has pulled us in the direction of defining who we are by the opinions of others and us *reacting* to what others say about us.

Anyone who engages daily with any social media knows that we are affected by many oppositional opinions and negative reactions to information that directly impact our minds, hearts, and souls.

We are left feeling anxious, disillusioned, lonely, and sometimes even *more conflicted*. These feelings can lead us toward alcohol and substance abuse, isolation, and any number of unhealthy behaviors that are anything but peaceful.

Even confident and strong-willed individuals can be negatively impacted by reading *just one* media post or reaction to something we've said online that is unkind and in disagreement with our views. No matter how we try to dismiss that comment; it can have power over us to negate anything positive.

This is not the way we were intended to live as we were created by our loving God to live in peace and harmony. This is not living life to the fullest, let alone one that is yielding the greatest tranquility.

Several years ago, I made the difficult decision to delete my primary social media account that I had built over two decades. It was tough at first to imagine the information from thousands of contacts I might miss, but I surprisingly felt peace and freedom after a small adjustment period.

I no longer felt drawn into viewing posts or commenting on posts that had no direct relevance in enhancing the quality of my life and relationships. I simply redirected my time and communication efforts by becoming much more proactive and attentive toward those people that were truly a priority.

That intentional effort deepened my relationships with my closest family members and friends; *my soul felt much more peaceful.* It was a life lesson that also impacted my family in more positive ways.

If we desire true peace and contentment, we should strive to seek out only positive interactions that are the healthiest for our souls with a *Christ-centric* conscience that directs all of our thoughts, intentions, and actions.

If peace is our ultimate goal, we may consider consistently asking, "Is this good for my soul?" and, "Is this best for the core foundation of my family?"

If the answer to these questions is not affirming our true identities, we need to ask God for the grace to keep our souls strong and *redirect* us into healthier directions.

The day I chose to replace my social media time investment with more spiritually enhancing activities was a healthier decision. I felt more peaceful and today, continue to enjoy more joy-filled relationships and moments with those I cherish.

In the book of Matthew 16:13-20, there's a profound story that directly addresses the value of respecting your core and knowing who you are. Jesus asked his apostles, "Who do others say I am and who do you say that I am?" It's an important foundational Bible story and was a defining moment at the beginning of His ministry.

Peter responded by saying, "You are the Messiah, the Son of the living God," (Matt. 16:16). Jesus felt reassured that Peter would become the rock and foundation upon which He would build His church. Jesus probably already knew what they thought, but He wanted and needed them to speak their truth confidently.

He wants us and needs us to speak our truth and to do the same today. He wants us to know *who He is* and *who we are* in relationship to Him. This knowledge brings tranquility to the core of our souls.

Sadly, many of us don't really know who we truly are, or we've forgotten who we are. We've become so accustomed to defining ourselves by what *we do* and how we perform for others. It's hard for us to just *be*.

We've lost our true sense of self because we live in a world filled with conflicting messages and we are drawn into that chaotic energy daily.

We are driven to achieve and not believe.

Truly believing we are children of a loving God who desires to live inside our souls *should* keep us grounded in this comforting truth. This truth, lived confidently each day, should offer peace.

The busyness of life gets in the way of this critical need for self-reflection. We truly need to set aside quiet time to reflect on these spiritual matters. This knowledge should be enough to give us the balance and harmony we seek in our daily interactions with others.

Unfortunately, this truth is drowned out by the constant demands of living in a materialistic and relativistic world that does not value faith-driven values.

If asked right now, "Who are you?" what would you say? That answer reflects how peacefully you are living and how you feel about your life. You are not at peace if the core of your soul is conflicted and you don't know who you truly are.

I recall an incident a few years ago when I invited a priest into my Confirmation classroom to talk to my students about the Sacrament of Reconciliation and how it should be a grace-filled and joyous occasion. They truly feared confessing their sins to a priest.

Most of my students had not received this sacrament since second grade. He opened the conversation by asking, "Who are you?" There was complete silence from the group of forty children. Not one child answered his question.

I felt so discouraged that the lessons I had taught them had not been retained. I was thinking, "Surely my kids know they are children of God!" That's the one message I reminded them of repeatedly every single week for months.

I realized that the priest had asked this question because he already knew they were afraid. He wanted to reassure them that as a priest, he was only acting on behalf of a truly loving Father. He wanted them to say that they were *a child of God*. He hoped they could embrace the joy and grace given in this sacrament without fear.

Fortunately, they all responded really well to his visit, proceeded to receive the sacrament that day and they loved the experience. One student enthusiastically said, "I feel so clean. I can't wait to go again!"

After the priest left the classroom, I asked them why they could not answer that one, simple question. One by one, they shared that they truly did not understand what he wanted of them. Unfortunately, each student thought he wanted to know *what they did* not who they were deep down inside their hearts and souls.

They didn't know how to connect with that question because they were so used to defining themselves as a son, daughter, brother, sister, student, athlete, or performer rather than who they were as a human being and child of God. Verbal communication for this group was extremely challenging.

They had become so accustomed to sharing their feelings, thoughts, and opinions via texting or some other smartphone application or social media platform. They were paralyzed to speak openly for fear of rejection or embarrassment.

That year, the program we were teaching was called *Chosen* by Ascension Press. Our goal was to instruct them in ways that would help them to explore who they were, why they were *chosen*, and how God wanted them to use their special gifts to make the world better.

It seemed plausible to me that these conversations might not be happening at home regularly or that their parents were challenged by trying to engage them as I was. I felt deeply moved by this realization and wanted to make a difference for them and their parents.

My passion as a teacher was to ensure that before they received the Sacrament of Confirmation, that they felt they were truly loved by God, and that every choice they made and challenge they faced in their lives would be filled with grace and joy if they believed without question: *Christ desired to live in their souls and they needed to invite Him in regularly.*

I knew then that those teaching them, guiding and caring for them at home, also had to believe that about *themselves*, first and foremost, before they could effectively guide their children. The core of our compass has to be Christ if we desire peace. Most of us do not feel this in our lives regularly.

Making this spiritual commitment offers transformational peace. As parents, caretakers, and educators, it's even more critical that we embrace a lifestyle with Christ as our core so that we can navigate our *own decisions* with a soul *that is steady and strong.*

Our children will consequently follow our lead and no matter what challenges get in the way of productive and positive choices. A core that is Christ-centric and a soul that is regularly strengthened with God's grace will direct our steps toward a faithful path of peace and joy without fear and worry.

IN THEIR HEARTS HUMANS PLAN
THEIR COURSE, BUT THE LORD
ESTABLISHES THEIR STEPS.
PROVERBS 16:9

COMPASS CONNECTIONS: Reflect on the following scripture passages and write down specific ways you can apply these messages to your plans of making better choices for **Christ as your Core** in your new Compass Club living strategy:

"In all your ways acknowledge him, and he will make your paths straight." - Proverbs 3:6

_____

_____

_____

_____

"Let the peace of Christ rule in your hearts, since as members of the one body you were called to peace. And be thankful." - Colossians 3:15

_____

_____

_____

_____

"God is love. Whoever lives in God, and God in him." - 1 John 4:16-17

_____

_____

_____

_____

"I am the true vine, and my Father is the vinedresser. Every branch in me that does not bear fruit He takes away, and every branch that does bear fruit He prunes, that it may bear more fruit. Already you are clean because of the word that I have spoken to you. Abide in me, and I in you. - John 15: 1-4

_____
_____
_____
_____

COMPASS COMMITMENT: This is what I will personally do to commit to implement the new ideas in this chapter that will strengthen my soul toward behaviors that reflect **Christ is my Core**.

1.

2.

3.

DIRECTING THE ARROW

This week I will write a love letter to God that shares how I am feeling about my life and my relationships. I will include areas I'd like to make a change, share my gratitude for the blessings I have in my life, and I will make a promise to make my faith journey a greater priority.

I will also review the time I invest each day with physical fitness, spiritual fitness, and social media. I will prayerfully discern ways I can achieve a better balance that is healthier for my soul.

JOURNAL REFLECTIONS FOR THE WEEK:

_____
_____
_____
_____
_____
_____
_____
_____
_____
_____
_____
_____
_____
_____
_____
_____
_____
_____
_____
_____
_____
_____
_____
_____

CHAPTER 2:

OTHERS: THE RELATIONSHIPS YOU CHOOSE

LUKE 6:12-13

"Jesus went out to the mountain to pray; and all night he continued in prayer to God. And when it was day, he called his disciples, and chose from them twelve, whom he named apostles."

As a young child, my mother would often share with me this one piece of advice when discussing my circle of friends, "You are who your friends are." I would continue to hear these words of wisdom in my head over the years when I had conflicts with friends or when I was entering into new social situations.

It was very helpful to me when I was discerning friends I'd choose to keep close and those I had to send away because they made me feel uncomfortable. Sometimes those decisions were excruciatingly painful.

The friends I wanted to have sometimes simply were not good for my soul and I innately knew that. I'm confident that those feelings came to me, not because I had a sixth sense about them, but because as a young girl, I was keeping close to God through my prayers and continually asking for grace, guidance, and direction.

The friends that I kept were those that empowered me to be my best self and did not tempt me to do or say things that were not good for me. The friends I chose were those that allowed me to be true to myself and authentic in my actions. I felt joy with those chosen friends and peace. I preferred this over the stress of trying to fit in with a crowd that wasn't a positive influence.

Sometimes, those friends that were fun or popular were not the ones making decisions that were honorable. Although I faced ridicule and embarrassment by not having them in my life, I did have to make those tough decisions to let them go. It was easier then because there were no cell phones, social media posts, and other technologies to further complicate the boundaries of formative relationships and friendships.

Even as an adult, I have had to continue to make these choices and those decisions are evolving. It's hard to know, with limited time available, where it's best to spend time and with whom. These decisions are critically important for the core of our being. Our decisions in this *others* quadrant directly impact how our children are making choices for their friends.

They are watching what we do and how we handle situations even if we are not aware of their observations. Our young children and teenagers sometimes do not share their feelings with us and are challenged to figure out how to cope on their own when they experience tough social situations.

The 'O' in our compass quadrant can have a dramatic impact on all the other areas of our life because like Jesus, we all need that close-knit core of *others* to keep us grounded in faith and making good life choices in all of our life quadrants.

Jesus also faced the fear of rejection and even bodily harm from his persecutors. Can you imagine the thousands of damaging posts He'd get on social media if He was online today? His apostles became His family; they protected Him and lifted Him during those times of self-doubt and isolation. There was a high degree of reciprocal love, respect, trust, and unconditional support between them when they traveled with Him during the years of His public ministry.

Even though Jesus had Mary, Joseph, and God, His heavenly Father and the apostles were His lifeline for His earthly mission. *Choosing others well* allowed Him to remain strong and intentionally directed toward His earthly life mission.

I've always thought the story of *how* Jesus chose His twelve apostles and closest friends was a story packed with rich lessons.

How He made His selections rather than *who* He chose is worth reflecting upon. The story could have been that God, His Father, knew what was best for His Son, so He selected the most important people who would build the foundation of His Son's ministry. You might imagine that the *very foundation* for our apostolic church, namely, one driven by the actions of twelve priests with one Pope would be a *critical* piece to our salvation story.

God, the Father, was a key advisor in this scenario, but He did not do the choosing. This advisory role He had with His Son is the *same role* He deeply desires to have with us today. Sometimes, we neglect to pray and invite Him into these important choices for ourselves.

Interestingly enough, if you reflect and reread the scripture passage from Luke 6:12-13, you'll notice that Jesus prayed all night into the early morning. Jesus was in direct and constant communication for at least *twelve consistent hours*, perhaps one hour for each apostle? His Father was truly guiding Him in the right direction of those that would be best for His Son's soul and the goals of His ministry.

He did not do this alone. Scripture doesn't say, "Jesus awoke from a peaceful slumber and God provided His important list of apostles." It was a critical time of intentional instruction that reflects the direct correlation of intense prayer to those He chose as His first priests.

His intimacy with His Father through prayer was what brought forth the grace to choose wisely. You could say that this is a model of how we should proceed in our lives with all of our important life decisions. How often do we neglect to pray about our choices in this quadrant of our lives?

The importance of *others* as a quadrant for the *Compass Club* was validated when I was teaching religious prep classes for Confirmation during my observation of the various student friend groups.

I intentionally did not assign the seats for my class of twenty-nine students. Interestingly enough, students always chose a seat with schoolmates even when they did not know them well. They all gravitated toward those they knew and went to great lengths to convince me that they *should* stay together.

What was fascinating to me, however, was that these children participated in *more positive ways* when they were not in small groups with *those* individuals. When they were with their peer group, they were *more disruptive* and engaged in attention-seeking activities.

Some would do anything they could to appear overly confident and aloof about being even slightly interested in anything I was teaching. These middle school children were uncomfortable sharing their feelings and doing or saying anything that would reflect their innermost thoughts, concerns, and fears. I had a few brave souls that would speak up, but for the most part, many resisted.

They could not initially connect with their hearts and souls to our lessons. It was very obvious that most of them were having a really hard time focusing on what I was saying because they actually preferred to be on their phones. They could not simply be still and enjoy time away from technology even for one hour.

I realized that I'd need to find ways to teach them how to feel safe when sharing their feelings with a great deal of patience and creativity. Even more importantly, I needed to help them understand how to be more aware of the strong gravitational pull of their material world.

Above all, teaching them that those social pressures that were pulling them away from their true selves were not in their best interest of living peacefully as chosen children of God. Choosing others who encouraged them to act *authentically* from a Christ-centric core became one of my most important mission-critical goals as their teacher.

Interestingly, I had more positive contributions with more reflective responses when I mixed up the groups. The social pressures of being with one's friend group did not bring out the best engagement from each individual. When I addressed this observation as a teacher, they told me that they were afraid to be judged and embarrassed by their friends for being too religious. The group mentality was so very different than the individual sharing with me that was very spiritually rich.

Their innermost feelings shared through their private notes to me in handouts I provided brought me to tears. Their deep longing to connect and share their true feelings was strong. Their insights shared were endearing and meaningful. They craved more intimacy but lacked the confidence to communicate their feelings for fear of being judged.

This gave me a unique opportunity to encourage them to *actively choose people* in their lives that made them feel comfortable. This meant teaching them to recognize people in their path that were not good for their souls and explaining how they could change that.

They needed strategies and courage to do the right thing. I focused on helping them to visualize a life of peace with genuine friends which was much healthier than the alternative life of being anxious with friends who did not honor their core.

As their teacher, I was consistently in a position to help them recognize the strong temptations in society that directed them away from peace and how they could make better choices. It became a consistent message I shared with them, but I knew that their parents, teachers, and caregivers needed to reinforce these lessons outside of my classroom.

My intention for each lesson was to remind them over and over again that each of them had been chosen by God to use their talents and gifts to make the world a better place. Furthermore, they needed to direct the arrow of their compass and guide their soul by moving in the direction that was most pleasing to God.

Surrounding themselves with people who made good decisions and life choices would give them extraordinary peace. It was hard to convince them that the health of their invisible souls was even *more important* than the bodies they could see. I saw the impact I had as a teacher, once a week, for nine months. I was hopeful that by writing this book, I could encourage those guiding them to continue this dialogue with them.

As parents and caretakers, I do believe that there are many subliminal messages *we* also send to our children relative to those *we choose* to be close to us. There were hints of this reality that my students shared with me about their family lives.

If we are using social media for hours at a time to make *connections* and not engaging in more intimate conversations with our friends and family members, we are sending conflicting messages to our impressionable children. What they see is more impactful than what they hear. We can't expect our children to see social media as a negative influence if we are not role modeling the behavior of them we desire.

Children do learn what they live.

It's critically important that we discern now, during these formative years with our children, how our behaviors model good habits we want them to adopt. Our own relationship with social media complicates our intention to discipline our children while we manage our own attachments.

We can't preach what we don't practice ourselves. Taking the time to truly assess how our children view our relationship choices will help you see the correlation to their decisions more clearly.

Today, we have access to so many more opportunities and access to a much larger global community impacting us as a result of technology. Those pressures can cause anxiety and even loneliness instead of the happiness and peace we seek or desire for ourselves and our families.

We know how we feel from one single media post that can threaten our self-esteem and confidence. Positive self-talk can't always erase a mean-spirited or ill-intentioned text that can linger in our minds. Imagine what our children are seeing and reading daily themselves and what they are not sharing with us.

Our children are spending hours of their day chatting with friends in virtual ways that lack the soul-fulfilling benefits of in-person conversations. These interactions, at times, are judgmental and hurtful, leaving impressionable comments online and in public that have immediate and long-term, damaging effects.

We are in a state of distress and conflict because we are trying to have formative engagement with our children but are competing with their screen time which is far more interactive and entertaining.

The technology we and our children are using thrives on instant gratification and speed. Much of this social activity is impulsive and does not have an objective decision-making focus. More than ever we have to understand what is pushing them in the direction of engaging in Snapchat, Instagram, YouTube, and other emerging technologies and virtual activities that do not offer any meaningful, *soul-enriching* energy.

Many of our children have thousands of friends who are *followers* who like their posts and pictures, but do they have any idea who they truly are? This passive, online activity is driving more loneliness and increasing alienation for our families. *This is not a path to peace.*

Some technologies do offer the efficacy of maintaining contact with a large network of friends and family members, but establishing *healthy boundaries* is truly necessary if we want our children to enjoy life-fulfilling relationships in this quadrant of their compass. If we allow the incessant activity to continue without an ongoing dialogue, we risk losing our children to influencers that offer toxic perspectives.

Their use of social media and its impact on their judgment is so much greater than what we experienced as children growing up. We need to find daily opportunities to talk to our children now more than ever before, so we can guide them toward those that are healthy for their souls and letting go of those relationships that are not pure and soul-enriching.

Knowing the "why" for their close friend choices is an important factor in preserving their mental stability and our own. As they grow and mature, they may be called upon to support those that need their help but choosing the healthiest souls as *influencers* is vital to their mental health in their early developmental years. The boundaries that we establish for our family lives may not be popular with our children but in the long term, we will be ensuring a clearer path to optimal mental health that is soul-fulfilling, not soul-depleting.

We also are a much more active generation with children that are engaging in sports and after-school activities on a far greater level and at *earlier ages* than years ago. Our friendship circles of influence are wider, bigger, and more demanding of our time and energy.

We can truly support healthier decisions if we talk to our children and share our thoughts as we are processing *decisions with our friendships and social situations*. This role modeling will have an immediate impact on how they are also evaluating their friend groups. The more you share with them, the more courageous they'll be when making the best choices for themselves.

These are teaching moments that we sometimes forget we have. It's vitally important today, especially now when the rates of suicide, depression, body image conflicts, and drug abuse are so high that we are acutely sensitive to the demands of connecting with our children.

They need and want to have meaningful connections and they can learn a great deal just by watching us. They want to hear from us even if they are not *asking* for those conversations. We have to initiate conversations about this quadrant of *others* more often.

As a parent, prayer has become a critical strategy for me over the years, particularly when I need guidance for these sensitive conversations. Seeking God's counsel has helped to facilitate more positive sharing of thoughts, feelings, and openness for my children to consider alternative ways of seeing my perspectives.

We sometimes forget that our role to guide means not only sharing our own past life experiences but also those life situations we continue to face every day. Our children need this emotional connection today more than ever. They need conversations with us, not strangers on smartphone applications.

They will relate and learn more from us when we can relate to them with positive encouragement. Children need to know we also felt conflict at their age and even now as adults. Our stories of vulnerability will comfort them and connect them to appropriate coping behaviors.

The *others* quadrant that includes us providing feedback can and will have a profound impact on the life direction your child takes. It's in our best interest to find ways to be included here as a key influencer who our children proactively choose for advice, not just because they are *obligated.*

By sharing our personal stories and past experiences with them, we will create a pathway to connect with authentic communication that brings peace to the family as a whole. Our children need to be reminded that *their* own life stories are evolving right now, and each chapter is being written by the relationships they choose.

If their engagement with influencers is primarily based on passive communication through social media and technology; they will not have a healthy sense of self to live the life story that God has already written on their hearts.

Even when our children appear distant or disinterested, we can still share with them our personal stories that we experienced during our childhood that may help to open up conversations. Our children will benefit when they see our vulnerability and hear how we overcame similar challenges growing up. Sharing with them these life lessons can empower them to share their situations as they are unfolding in their social circles.

The seeds that God has planted in our souls and those of our children need strong soil and cultivation to grow and produce the finest fruit, so gifts are shared. Friendships we cultivate are the key to that nourishment.

We need to teach our children the importance of keeping their souls fed and moving in the direction of only those or *others* who are truly going to make that journey a wonderful story. When good souls connect, there is immeasurable happiness and tranquility to the soul. When the heart is conflicted, it's usually because the right souls are not in sync with one another.

Unfortunately, today, our children are not capable of assigning the proper value to events that transpire between them and their many friends; sometimes thousands of friends on social media. Events are moving too quickly for them to discern what is authentic.

The healthy development of their true selves depends on navigating this quadrant well. We love our children and above all, we want them to love themselves and be lifted by others who encourage and validate their self-worth especially when we cannot be with them.

Cultivating this practice and intention in your family life may feel very different, but well worth the consideration. *Peace will ensue in everyone's hearts.* You'll worry less about their choices. Don't forget to invite God into these times of discernment for your friendships.

The grace that comes to your life from this reliance on God will be transformative and will teach your children invaluable life lessons that will stay with them through adulthood. You will be ensuring a legacy of peace and joy that changes your family life forever.

COMPASS CONNECTIONS: Reflect on the following scripture passages and write down specific ways you can apply these messages to your plans of making better choices for **Others** in your new Compass Club living strategy:

"Make no friendship with a man given to anger, nor go with a wrathful man, lest you learn his ways and entangle yourself in a snare." - Proverbs 22:24-25

_____
_____
_____
_____

"Greater love has no one than this, that someone lay down his life for his friends. You are my friends if you do what I command you. No longer do I call you servants, for the servant does not know what his master is doing; but I have called you friends, for all that I have heard from my Father I have made known to you." - John 15: 13-15

_____
_____
_____
_____

"A friend loves at all times, and a brother is born for a time of adversity." - Proverbs 17:17

_____
_____
_____
_____

"And let us consider how to stir up one another to love and good works, not neglecting to meet together, as is the habit of some, but encouraging one another, and all the more as you see the day drawing near." - Hebrews 10:24-25

COMPASS COMMITMENT: This is what I will personally do to commit to embracing the new ideas in this chapter that will strengthen my soul in the direction of **Choosing Others** that reflect that **Christ is my Core.**

1.

2.

3.

DIRECTING THE ARROW

This week I will make a list of all my friends and acquaintances who interact with me on a regular basis either personally or on some social media platform. I will commit to creating *three lists* of those that are healthy for my soul, those that are not positive influencers, and those that are not on that list that perhaps *should be.*

I will *pray* before making these lists and ask the Holy Spirit to enlighten my mind and heart to discern the truth and give me the grace to make better choices moving forward. I will commit to investing quality time with those that share my values and lift my spirits. I will courageously find a way to let go of those relationships that take away my peace, but I will continue to pray for them

JOURNAL REFLECTIONS FOR THE WEEK

_____
_____
_____
_____
_____
_____
_____
_____
_____
_____
_____
_____
_____
_____
_____
_____
_____
_____
_____
_____
_____
_____

CHAPTER 3:

THE MORAL COMPASS: MODESTY AND MORALITY

Philippians 4:8

"Finally, brothers, whatever is true, whatever is honorable, whatever is just, whatever is pure, whatever is lovely, whatever is commendable, if there is any excellence, if there is anything worthy of praise, think about these things."

We are living in a perpetual state of crisis management when it comes to this quadrant. Our society values sexual permissiveness over modesty and morality. Choices concerning ethical and moral dilemmas made today are often relative to how one *feels* in the moment.

Manufacturers, retail buyers, and trending stylists continue to make it very difficult to buy clothing that is not designed to be provocative, sexually enticing, and morally compromising.

Popular social media is flooded with images of teens, young adults, and influential celebrities who dress scantily, speak irreverently, and behave in disrespectful ways. Parents are being forced to have very mature conversations about sexuality and modesty with their youngest and most vulnerable children much earlier than ever. Social situations that negatively impact our children's mental health force us to be even more hyper-vigilant with social media than ever before.

Even young girls who are trying to live moral lifestyles and dress modestly are bombarded with popular fashion images that are not reflective of what is wholesome and pure.

The daily influx of provocative social media that drives the most *likes* creates a *new reality* that causes harmful peer pressure on our impressionable children. Our sons are being tempted with sexual images of women that make them also feel confused and conflicted.

When my daughter was in elementary school, I held a *pure* fashion show and fundraising event for girls in fourth through sixth grades at a local country club. We had a young, female Christian artist who promoted a positive message of modesty for her lifestyle music platform.

The girls were asked to select and model only clothing that was *pure* fashion and most reflective of their own unique and personal style. The parents and their daughters had the opportunity to shop together and have discussions about why they should not promote inappropriate attention to their bodies.

It was a challenge to find age-appropriate and modest choices, but the process was a good one. By not succumbing to the peer pressure of finding what was popular and more easily accessible; they each selected unique outfits to model that were not replicated. It took a bit longer to shop but the experience was invaluable.

Each girl's style shone through on the stage and they felt empowered. It was a life experience that positively impacted them toward making better choices in their later years. They learned valuable lessons for staying true to their core by not following the trends.

We need more opportunities like this and more dialogue between parents and their children while they are still in these critical and formative years of discernment. The world tells them what's in style, but that's not what God wants for the peace of their soul.

What is popular and promiscuous can cause a loss of *pure* and honorable self-expression resulting in feelings of anxiety and loss of identity. Staying on a pure path connected to one's soul where Christ lives with a strong conscience will consistently guide the best choices.

It's our responsibility to find creative ways to instill these intrinsic self-worth values consistently. The gravitational pull of these toxic influences will only get stronger the older our children get so now is the time to establish honorable goals for your family.

When your children become teens and young adults, the foundation of this quadrant will be solid if their path was virtuous. They will be more capable of navigating their own compass independently and confidently.

It's important that we pause and reflect on our own expression of modesty and morality in our adult lives and what those appearances communicate to the children we are trying to lead.

Any manner in which we speak, dress, or act that invites sinful thoughts or actions is not a peaceful disposition for our soul and it does not respect the sanctity of others. Loving ourselves and loving others is made more possible when we cherish our bodies and minds in the purest fashion as God intended when He created us.

It can be truly challenging and stressful to find a balance for our cultural attitudes as parents when we are *simultaneously* trying to guide those that depend on us. Socially charged situations come up often today when we are pressured to provide a reasonable response to our children's behaviors that conflict with the moral foundations we've created in our homes.

In matters of the heart and soul where *moral or ethical* dilemmas surface, those times can cause stress and anxiety in our most important relationships. Satan thrives on fear and chaos and there's no area of our compass where temptation and sin thrive more than areas of moral discernment and modest behaviors.

Taking time to pray, reflect, and wait to respond is so necessary to keep peace in your soul and your home. Modesty is a virtue that needs constant cultivation through prayer as a first-most priority. You can't live and survive as someone with pure intentions without it. Modesty has to become a deliberate way of life.

Intention will drive the energy to act with conviction.

Technological access to provocative and immoral views from more liberal-minded influencers makes it so arduous to stay on the holy path. Navigating our moral compasses let alone guiding our families toward God's truth require tenacity and fearlessness. This quadrant represents the most dynamic area with the greatest potential for family unrest and distress.

Today more than ever, discussions of what is modest and moral can become a heated battlefield with those we cherish the most. Sometimes we don't have clear directives when we pray, and decisions have to be made faster than we have the patience or luxury of waiting for clarity from above.

We are conflicted when it comes to what is honorable today and what guidelines for modesty seem to be reasonable without being too old-fashioned in our beliefs.

Many of us want to be relevant, emotionally available, and approachable by our children as they mature, but we don't want to sacrifice our moral values when they push boundaries due to their peer pressures. We want strong family relationships but recognize that sometimes, differences in opinions toward societal norms are going to be different than how we grew up, how we want to live, and how we want our children to behave.

Finding the right balance of trying to engage in conversations that are productive and peaceful, but also upholding our family values and virtuous ideals is not easy. It's so critical, however if you want to preserve the sanctity of your moral identity.

Morality and modesty are relative today in a liberal world where so many liberal social media influences contradict the more conservative advice we give to our young children or those we've already raised. What's deemed modest dress or honorable speech is being diluted over time. What was an R-rated movie long ago is now being shown to our younger children who are under eighteen years of age.

Not too long ago, a parent told me, "There's just a few curse words and not that much sex," as she justified her decision to let her younger child watch a controversial film that many felt was too inappropriate. I had another parent tell me a few years ago,

"I'll just have her close her eyes when it gets to a bad part that's not age-appropriate," because she really wanted to see the movie and didn't have a babysitter.

Many of us feel overwhelmed simply by keeping up with the ever-consuming demands of living our lives and juggling so many priorities. Sometimes, we are just too tired. We feel tempted to just give up and give in.

Online movie networks like Netflix, Hulu, Amazon Prime Video, Peacock, HBO, and other numerous up-and-coming networks are producing movies at an increasing rate. These mediums have minimal filters for bad language, provocative themes, and exposure to nudity and sexual images that are impacting the safe parenting boundaries.

There might be software programs out there that offer safety and protection, but that doesn't keep us in close relationships with our children. Connecting with our children and inviting them to actively and openly discuss what they are watching and how they feel about what they are viewing is the only way to instill virtues that last.

We hope the virtuous foundations we've provided to our families are strong to stand the test of time, but once our children are out of our reach, the strong gravitational pull of worldly influences that promote a dress code and a more modern view of what's morally honorable is left to weaken the parental bonds.

We desire to stay strong in our own moral beliefs, but temptations surface, and the soul is weakened. The gravitational forces that drive very liberal ways of thinking and behaving cause unrest in our family relationships all too often.

It's become increasingly hard to keep up with the pressures, but we must persist if we want peaceful and virtuous relationships. This might be the most frustrating quadrant of the compass for all of us, *perhaps the most unsettling.*

It's normal for children to want to experiment and desire independence from us. Today, this issue of morality and modesty is in constant danger of being something we can't enforce because the world has too many toxic influencers that pervade social media platforms. Their styles of provocative dress and irreverent communication threaten healthy, family bonds.

Our impressionable children are seeing these influencers wearing seductive clothing, hearing perverse language, and seeing movies and commercials that challenge our wholesome virtues. We can't possibly monitor thousands of images delivered from YouTube videos, TikTok, and texts that our children are viewing on any given day. It's a world that we did not experience in our developmental years.

Today, women are increasingly *encouraged* to show their strength and independence by proudly showing *more* of their bodies. This freedom of expression without healthy boundaries promulgates sin and temptation for the soul. This mentality without proper parental guidance can lead to low self-esteem and identity confusion.

Empowerment that highlights your self-worth through the immodest expression of your body over the purity of your mind creates confusion in relationships. It's a mindset that diminishes the value of the soul and places more value on what's on the outside. Unfortunately, purity is not fashionable in our modern world today.

Today, it's popular and *on-trend* to freely show more sacred body parts and to be proud of that expression of freedom. Many parents are tired of fighting and give in to the idea that, "It is what it is," and "That's the way our world is now." This is not how God intended our bodies to be respected. Popular media disagrees. We can't stay silent in this battle of wills.

There are two ways of managing this issue; hope for the best that our children will eventually find their way *or* continue to insist on the obedience of our expectations as parents for respectful behavior. Above all, we must continue to instill and affirm our faith values with our children often.

Teaching them again and again that God's will is to love Him above all others and love our neighbors as ourselves. This expression of love should be pure.

God gave us *purity of heart* as a gift to cherish at Baptism that is made visible when we honor the body and soul. An arrow that stays strong in the *modesty* and *morality* quadrant allows perfect love to flourish in all of our relationships and tranquility is achieved. Immodesty does cause lust, temptation, and sinfulness toward our neighbor.

We are not honoring the sacredness of the soul of our neighbor if we are not behaving honorably. If we demand compliance and adoption of our views, we worry that we'll destroy our family relationships. You can only place restrictions for so long. It's really hard to uphold moral standards when the rest of the world doesn't support your views. These are tough situations and challenging times for sure.

Unfortunately, those that favor the sanctity of the soul over the modern trends are the minority. Pure intentions are not always popular. We can't fight this battle without inviting the Holy Spirit into our lives consistently to guide the best intentions for our souls and the protection of our families. We need to remain *prayerful and courageous.*

When we go back to scripture, we will find great comfort and timely advice for this quadrant. In Matthew 5:3-12, we have the very first and *most impactful* sermon that Jesus gave to thousands at the Sermon on the Mount. These words shared over two thousand years ago summarize the core foundation of His message for His followers as the Son of God, but they are equally relevant for our parenting purposes today.

He called these guidelines The Beatitudes as the perfect way to live faithfully and *remain blessed.*

Blessed are the poor in spirit,
   for theirs is the kingdom of heaven.

Blessed are those who mourn,
   for they will be comforted.

Blessed are the meek,
   for they will inherit the earth.

Blessed are those who hunger and thirst for righteousness,
  for they will be filled.

Blessed are the merciful,
  for they will be shown mercy.

Blessed are the pure in heart,
  for they will see God.

Blessed are the peacemakers,
  for they will be called children of God.

Blessed are those who are persecuted because of righteousness,
  for theirs is the kingdom of heaven.

Blessed are you when people insult you, persecute you and falsely
say all kinds of evil against you because of me.

The priority Jesus gave to *purity* for these eight beatitudes was *very
high*. The only beatitude that allows you to *see God* is to remain
pure in spirit. Purity has to be an intentional way of life that comes
from the heart and soul united.

For most Christians, seeing the face of God is our ultimate goal
in life; to have lived a life worthy of our calling and to spend
salvation with Him. *Purity in spirit* needs to be a vocation we live
fearlessly and with great conviction if we desire the peaceful path
to Jesus, Himself.

The *Catechism of the Catholic Church* also offers great insights here:

Purity requires modesty, an integral part of temperance. Modesty
protects the intimate center of the person. It means refusing to
unveil what should remain hidden. It is ordered to chastity to
whose sensitivity it bears witness. It guides how one looks at
others and behaves toward them in conformity with the dignity
of persons and their solidarity. [2]

Modesty will naturally evolve from this disposition of conformity
because nothing that *contradicts* an intention to do God's will and
to live virtuously will feel peaceful.

No outside influences that negate the virtues of living this way will have power over a soul that lives in God's truth. The culture of today that promotes sinful attraction by words and clothing will have no power against a soul united with Christ as the core.

Honoring the body in words and actions strengthens the soul and brings the peace of Christ to the mind. Those that live this way are not insecure, restless, nor struggling with feelings of low self-worth. Knowing who you are and who lives inside you as a pure vessel of grace should bring great comfort and confidence.

We truly need to make conscious decisions as faithful families to *consistently* instill and reinforce our moral expectations. We need to highlight the dangers of immodesty and impurity for as long as we have this strong influence over our children. We simply cannot give up this mission to stay on the path to purity that offers peace to our souls.

These conversations in the home are critically important now because issues related to low self-esteem and poor body image can and will lead to emotional distress for our young especially. These sinful thoughts and corresponding behaviors will rob one's soul of peace.

We must reinforce these lessons with our children that an intentional decision to remain pure in mind, heart, and soul embraces the dignity of the soul of others as well.

This generation is being mentally programmed and conditioned to show more of their bodies as a way to sell a *positive body image* that promotes confidence. Showing more of one's intimate body is supposed to represent freedom of expression.

The confusion with this way of thinking is that much of our youth do not realize that this so-called liberation leads to damaging and dangerous perceptions of their intrinsic value as women and men of God.

There's no freedom in representing one's humanity in a manner that disrespects the soul. This ideology can cause others to focus more on the physical body than the emotional well-being of the soul.

Body dysmorphia is a mental illness that has become a serious issue today for families with so many of our young obsessed with perceived flaws on their bodies. Their opinions have been shared by what they see online, in the movies, and through various social media platforms.

They've become overwhelmed and depressed about these ideals of body perfection that are simply unrealistic. Anorexia and bulimia are also and equally alarming conditions that have only heightened in severity as a result of this societal preoccupation with body perfection as well as sexually charged and permissive behaviors.

We know this way of living contributes to stress, loneliness, depression, and isolation for adults as well. This gravitational pull of the world is real and brings controversial and tough conversations into the home. You are either facing this challenge now or will be sure to experience this as your children get older.

I've raised my daughter in this *Compass Club* mentality since she was a small child, so I'm very fortunate to have a strong relationship with her that allows us to have open communication. Discussing options is a frequent exchange we have, but those discussions are not always easy.

I remain firm in my expectations and concerns about the "what ifs" of making poor choices. Connecting the dots between the sacredness of the body and the sanctity of the soul is a consistent theme in our conversations. She has always been very modest, yet she has become infinitely more challenged as she's matured.

She loves fashion, but everything that is trending right now promotes clothing styles that are very revealing and provocative. The styles have changed so drastically.

The styles that our children view on social media, posts by friends, celebrities, and popular stylists reflect strong dispositions that *immodesty and sexual liberation is the new normal.* So many fashions today highlight and accentuate excessive nudity.

Our daughters are being viewed more often as objects for pleasure than who they truly are as daughters of God. Their intellect, talents, gifts, and intrinsic worth as human beings are being devalued over time. Our sons are equally conflicted because their judgment of what they view doesn't really mirror the heart and soul of these women.

The future of healthy relationships and moral family life is vulnerable to these impure foundations. There's little authenticity being reflected in these social situations. The future mental and spiritual health of all of our important relationships and family life is in jeopardy.

The sheer pressure of keeping up with this *false image* externally is a key reason why so many of our youth have issues around drug and alcohol use accompanied by eating disorders. They are too often seeking outward validation from strangers for internal self-worth. Alarming statistics validate that low self-esteem is heightened as a result of misguided body images that are promoted on social media. This trajectory is dangerous.

It takes great strength of character and courage today to go against the popular majority. Furthermore, we know that dressing immodestly actually draws more negative attention and rarely if ever can instill long-lasting confidence. The only peaceful disposition that makes logical sense upholds God's truth with His commandments and beatitudes as scaffolding for our holy bodies as *temples of His grace*.

On the contrary, those that try to promote nudity and immodest dress or speech as signs of positive body image and female empowerment are confused. These people do not truly understand, true peace of mind comes naturally from virtuous activities that respect the mind, body and soul.

Admittedly, I have had to adjust my expectations at times and seek alternative ways to compromise, but the ongoing and daily dialogue with my children is the most critical part of this prayerful discernment.

God's free will has been given to our children and we must pray often that our conversations and their consciences guide them to choosing well in this quadrant. The conversations are going to be uncomfortable at the time, but if we truly want to *see God, purity in* purity *in spirit is a non-negotiable goal and way of life.*

I often hear from my children, their friends, and even good parents I know, "Well, that's in style right now; that's the look, what can we do if they are all doing it?"

The *Catechism of the Catholic Church* reminds us that "Purification of the heart demands prayer, the practice of chastity, purity of intention and *vision.*"[2532]

Vision here is the key component of what should empower us with the conviction of doing the right thing in all circumstances. Even if everyone is being sinful or putting themselves in a position to be harmed or judged wrongly, we as parents must act with honor and purity of intention at all times.

It's impossible to stay on the path to purity without a dedicated prayer life that calls on the Holy Spirit to send the grace for courageous convictions and decisions.

Many of us are facing our worst nightmare of becoming *social life enforcers.* Social media is toxic, powerful, and pervasive and it's only getting more sophisticated in how the technology *personalizes viewing behaviors and tendencies.* The gravitational pull is strong on all of our compasses.

Perseverance is the key. If we remain strong in upholding our truths, morals, and convictions, *our children will follow.* We all desire to raise confident, independent, and good-hearted people who are capable of making respectful life choices without us as they mature.

Living in fear and worry as a parent, however, is much more painful than living in trust and love knowing that the foundation and core have already been established and solidified. Trusting God to lead us and trusting ourselves to guide them needs to be *our vision.*

Times can change, but we must still uphold our moral values of virtuous living. We are educating our children with the best of everything: schools, coaches, and tutors so they are strong in their minds to make the best choices for their futures.

Why then would we ever foster an acceptance of any immodest behaviors for our middle school and teenage children that diminish the values of intelligence, communication, and healthy relational behaviors? If what we wear is the focus of how we feel about ourselves, then we should all be making intentional decisions that reflect *only* virtuous, honorable, and the purest choices.

These outside influencers won't disappear, so we must empower ourselves and our children now to navigate our and their respective compasses toward healthy and life-sustaining behaviors even if we face rejection, ridicule, mockery, or are ousted from friend groups.

Just recently, I was approached by a middle-aged saleswoman who gave me a dress she selected for prom consideration that she was sure I'd love for my daughter because she said, "It's really sexy!" I looked at her with sheer astonishment. I said, "No thank you, sexy is not what we were aiming for. My daughter is sixteen!"

We will never regret living a pure intentioned and modest lifestyle as a leader and trendsetter versus a follower. You never know *where and when* you'll need to step out in faith. That day, I was a witness not just for my daughter, but also for all the other mothers and daughters in the dressing room of that store. I can only hope those parents and their daughters were able to reflect more thoughtfully on their own choices that day.

Those that remain true to their core, will have no regrets long term when faced with temptations to follow the crowd. Short-term pleasure should not be valued higher than the long-term benefits of being respected in your choices of how you dress and speak.

I did face ridicule as a teenager because I was less tolerant of more provocative behaviors. I was left out of social gatherings and rejected. I eventually did find *others* who shared my faith, my morals, but it was not always an easy journey.

I learned then and I know now that it is more peaceful to surround yourself with those that inspire and lift you toward a moral lifestyle if you ultimately desire the healthiest mental stability. Every day we can exercise our free will to choose better and even when we fail, our merciful Father remains understanding and forgiving. He will always redirect us to a better path toward holiness.

Social media is *manic media* right now and only getting more challenging. God must be invited often into our family discussions. If we don't invite Him into our conversations and our life decisions, our children will not either.

The arrow of our soul can only stay focused with intentional prayer and the grace of God. We can't pray for His protection of our children if we or they are choosing to dress and behave in ways that invite sinfulness and vulnerability.

God is not a fixer.

He's given each of us free will and a code of conduct in the directives of the Ten Commandments. He's there to support our good choices and gladly lift us when we invite His intercession. His merciful love knows no boundaries when we fall from grace.

We hear often, "God has a plan," but how can we follow it or know it if we are not asking Him to guide us in this important quadrant?

In situations that invite controversy in this quadrant, we need to be courageous and speak openly with our children, "What would God do?" "How do you think God would think about this decision?" "Is this honorable in God's eyes?"

The *Compass Club* lifestyle encourages us to be true to our core, keep friends who support a moral lifestyle, and keep God first in our lives to guide all our choices.

If we adhere to this way of living ourselves, our children will follow our example more so than if we mandate or try to control the manner we want them to live. If we are not being moral in our actions or modest in our dress and speech; we can't expect respectful modeling from those entrusted to our care.

Grace will always be stronger than the world's gravitational pull on our compass. Grace makes peaceful decisions and purposeful living the most possible. The family will unravel if God is not permitted to lead with a daily invitation through a dedicated prayer life.

We must persevere for ourselves and those we love for the protection of our souls and those we cherish. Taking the time to analyze, review, and perhaps reinforce your moral code and engage in meaningful conversations as a family has never been more important in our world than right now.

A firm resolve in this quadrant of modesty and morality does not waiver. When your circle of influence are people who share your faith by embracing a pure code of conduct; you will feel a sustaining peace within. This one simple phrase, "Is this good for your soul?" will always best direct the path to holiness as God intended.

COMPASS CONNECTIONS: Reflect on the following scripture passages and write down specific ways you can apply these messages to your plans for making better **Moral and Modest** choices as part of your new Compass living strategy:

"Or do you not know that your body is a temple of the Holy Spirit within you, whom you have from God? You are not your own, for you were bought with a price. So, glorify God in your body." - 1 Corinthians 6:19-20

_____

_____

_____

_____

"I appeal to you therefore, brothers, by the mercies of God, to present your bodies as a living sacrifice, holy and acceptable to God, which is your spiritual worship. Do not be conformed to this world, but be transformed by the renewal of your mind, that by testing you may discern what is the will of God, what is good and acceptable and perfect." - Romans 12:12

_____

_____

_____

_____

"Do not be deceived: "Bad company ruins good morals." - 1 Corinthians 15:33

_____

_____

_____

_____

"Do not love the world or the things of the world. If anyone loves the world, the love of the Father is not in him. For all that is in the world, sensual lust, enticement for the eyes and the pretentious life, is not from the Father but is from the world. Yet the world and its enticement are passing away. But whoever does the will of God remains forever." - 1 John 2: 12-17

_____

_____

_____

_____

COMPASS COMMITMENT: This is what I will personally do to commit to embracing the new ideas in this chapter that will direct my soul toward **Moral and Modest** activities that reflect **Christ is my Core.**

1.

2.

3.

DIRECTING THE ARROW

This week I will review all of my social media accounts, my music playlists, and my wardrobe. I will delete or remove things that are not the *most* moral and modest choices. I know that when Christ is invited to support my choices of music, clothing and social media, these things should reflect *what brings me closer to Him* not farther away. What stays and what should go away? I know by doing this I will positively impact the souls of others by my good example.

JOURNAL REFLECTIONS FOR THE WEEK:

_____

_____

_____

_____

_____

_____

_____

_____

_____

_____

_____

_____

_____

_____

_____

_____

_____

_____

_____

_____

CHAPTER 4:

PRAYER POWER: FIRST THINGS FIRST

Luke 11:1-13

Now Jesus was praying in a certain place, and when he finished, one of his disciples said to him, "Lord, teach us to pray, as John taught his disciples." And he said to them, "When you pray, say: "Father, hallowed be your name. Your kingdom come. Give us each day our daily bread, and forgive us our sins, for we ourselves forgive everyone who is indebted to us. And lead us not into temptation."

In chapter one, we talked about the importance of working the *core* as part of a strong, physical fitness regimen. Anyone who has ever taken a fitness class, watched a training video, or had a personal trainer knows that engaging your core muscles is necessary to enjoy the full effects of the exercise and remain injury-free.

No one can actually *see* the core working, but by creatively visualizing the movement and tightening of the abdominal muscles, the core is strengthened and the internal engagement of those muscle groups and overall balance is achieved.

The same process can and should be applied to the *prayer process*. By doing the work of exercising your mind and formulating the intentions of *connecting your soul* to God through prayer, you are deepening your relationship with Him and strengthening your spiritual core.

By creatively visualizing a conversation between Father and child;

you will be *exercising* an intimate dialogue without really seeing but understanding that the process is working simply because you have the intention and are *investing time* to do the work. Prayer is a conscious decision and desire to connect intimately with God.

Prayer is the surest path to holiness if you want an authentic relationship and deeper connection with God. It's the one thing we can do that isn't about performing well. It's a nice break from the expectations the world places on us to do things perfectly. *It's a sure path to peace.*

With daily practice and consistent exercise, it will become a natural habit you will develop that becomes the ultimate source of your tranquility. Like any good habit that is worthwhile, it will take time to embrace this daily regimen. The power that comes from this commitment to pray will be felt immediately *in every quadrant* of your compass.

One recommendation for a sustainable practice is to begin your day following this process using a simple *GOD* acronym I find helpful: 'G' for gratitude, 'O' for opportunities, and 'D' for direction. This daily ritual has been a transformative blessing in my life.

Here's the formula. Simply reach out to your loving Father with *gratitude* in your heart for living another day. Ask Him for those *opportunities* that could be placed before you to serve Him better and make a difference in our world. Then, implore His *direction* for your day, ensuring that you invest the proper time to tasks that are most in accordance with *His divine will*, not your own.

Continue this dialogue throughout the day and then before you close your eyes at night; speak to God as if He's right there beside you. At night you can share your *gratitude* again for the blessings of the day, ask *forgiveness* for the mistakes you've made that day, and then *praise* God for His merciful love. Lastly, ask God for His almighty protection of your family, friends, and for healing for those that are not well.

You'll find more centeredness and internal peace because you have made this practice an integral part of your life. You will not feel alone during your day because you will be constantly checking in with God and asking for support, especially when your day might not be going so smoothly.

This discipline of prayer practice like physical exercise is something that provides so much greater clarity to busy parents and caregivers who are juggling so many priorities. Time is a precious commodity these days and the challenge to complete our many tasks seems endless and overwhelming.

Investing time with your Creator in daily prayer will provide clearer vision, a heavenly perspective, and sometimes, a redirection of your plans and efforts in ways you never thought possible.

I only wish I had understood the power of prayer back in those early days of my personal and career development. I'm almost certain the trajectory of my career, my relationship choices, and my life plans would have taken a much different turn. At a minimum, my stress level would have been much lower.

Prayer has become that single constant practice that strengthens my soul. By creating frequent opportunities to have an ongoing dialogue with God, I feel more confident that my prayers are heard. I'm able to know and feel that God has interceded because I am more relaxed and open to His intercession.

I feel comforted when I do ask for something specific that I desire for myself, my loved ones, or even strangers. Even when I do not receive something exactly as I had hoped, I just accept it wasn't God's will or timing and *I'm still at peace.*

This is a phenomenal benefit of an intentional prayer life. My prayers are very intimate and sometimes, quite casual as if I was talking to a close friend. I'm not always asking for things that are life-threatening or serious.

My request might be that He help me stay strong with my plan to eat healthier or help me navigate a challenging family situation. I might ask for support with my marriage when my husband and I are at an impasse when it comes to raising our children.

I might be struggling with my day and not sure how to prioritize my overwhelming to-do list. No request is too big or too small for God. He's become a trusted friend whom I know is *so grateful* I'm making time for Him.

Once I understood how much it truly comforted Him to have a relationship with me and talk with me, I wanted to do it all the time. Prayer is that gateway to peace and the glue that keeps me stuck to Him. I'm now able to feel a more intimate understanding of what He plans and hopes for me.

I've made so many decisions over the last few years based on thoughts that came to me in quiet moments of prayer that were completely opposed to what *I would have done* otherwise without praying. I have learned the invaluable life lesson of *taking everything to prayer before making decisions*. It's become a game-changer for me professionally, personally, and in all of my family relationships and friendships.

I realize it's hard to set aside time to pray because we are all so busy with endless lists of things to do that all seem to require immediate action. I used to use the Franklin Planner time management system when I was working in my career.

The system segmented tasks by categories classified as A1, A2, B1, B2, C1, C2, and so on. A's required immediate attention, B's would be secondary items that would be nice to get done, and C's could be comfortably moved to the next day or week.

Prayer in this instance always gets the A1 designation every day and often throughout the day. Giving my prayer life an A1 priority has provided the grace I've needed to allocate the proper level of priority, time, and attention to *everything else on my list*.

Prayer sometimes can be an afterthought or what we do when we *really need help*. We tend to prioritize activities that bring an immediate reward for our investment of time. Prayer doesn't typically have an immediate and definitive outcome that we can see with our own eyes. *We are impatient human beings*.

Prayer also requires a quiet disposition, but our lives are so very hectic. The opportunity to re-think the investment of time to pray is *now*. The promise of more peaceful living depends on finding frequent and contemplative opportunities to seek God through a prayerful dialogue that deepens our relationship with Him.

We need to take the time and find a sacred place in our lives that is non-negotiable. Our future peace of mind and sanctity of our souls are dependent on this decision. If our health or bodies were at risk of being harmed or injured, we would do everything possible to be proactive. Our souls need the same value and commitment to prayer.

Today, there is a fast-growing focus on the power of meditation as a way to relieve stress and anxiety. Yoga classes, meditation videos, podcasts, articles, and books are in high demand. Meditation practices focus on breath and relaxation techniques that support the balance of the mind, body, and spirit.

Investing *time to pray* embraces these same practices and goals and offers even greater and *sustainable* peace. When you make time to meditate with God as your partner, His grace transforms your mind, body, and soul. No one knows what your soul needs better than the Father who formed you.

As Catholics, we were taught as children to memorize prayers that became our path toward embracing our faith at mass, home, or at school. Traditionally, the Catholic prayers I learned fell into four types: *Adoration* (praising God), *Contrition* (asking God's forgiveness), *Petition* (asking God for a favor), and *Thanksgiving* (showing God gratitude).

I look back at my early prayer life and see that reciting these prayers in these categories was the way to pray. I never really *prayed* the prayers but merely *recited* them. I never took the time to meditate or reflect on the actual meaning of the words and feel the true benefits.

Why we prayed was not reinforced as much as *how* we did it. The truth be told, the prayers I recited were mostly *petition,* asking for things I thought I needed or wanted. I wasn't exactly using prayer as a way to grow closer to God.

It wasn't until much later in my life that I began to understand that communication with God, Jesus, the Blessed Mother Mary, and the saints can't be assessed on earthly terms. The give and take of communication in a relationship can be seen and felt easily. There's immediate validation to what we are saying by the visual cues and affirmations.

We have become frustrated over the years with prayer because we approach it like other earthly tasks and measure its impact and effectiveness by human assessment. This quadrant of prayer will become the unifying force for all other areas of life focus with a different approach, a little patience, and a dedicated spirit.

We simply must invest consistent time in this quadrant if we truly desire inner peace. To experience prayer as a treasury of grace is life's greatest blessing. Prayer guides our steps on the path to peace. The soul that is consistently directed toward this quadrant as an intentional activity will be strengthened.

To have an intimate relationship with Christ requires faith, trust, and daily action through prayer. It requires repetition and commitment to continue the practice and perfect the practice even if you're not sure what you are hearing back. Every day I'm praying, all the time.

Prayer that is the most endearing to me is when I'm just sitting in silence and sharing my gratitude for my faith and my life. There are many times I want to ask for favors, but it's rare because I feel confident God knows exactly what I need. God invites all forms of prayer without judgment.

I'm quick to ask for special considerations or favors only if when granted they are in complete alignment with God's will and not my own. I know that God is always going to give me what I need not always what I want and in *His time*.

When I hear people say they'll keep someone in their prayers, I wonder if they really will. Is this just something we say to be kind and supportive or are we really, with a sincere heart, going to the Father and truly praying for those intentions?

I have found that those people that share a passion for prayer tend to all reflect the same attributes. They exude a quiet, yet humble confidence in their personality. They reflect peace, trust, humility, acceptance, and love in the way they communicate with others. They are what I call *prayer warriors*.

These warriors live in the moment without fear of the future. They are trusting souls. They know that God is near and there's a beautiful exchange of frequent dialogue. They feel that their life is blessed even when there is great suffering and crosses that accompany that journey.

They seek opportunities for communal prayer at mass, retreats, bible studies, and book clubs to be strengthened in their dedication to this practice and to be lifted by other like-minded people. When they say, "I'll keep you in my prayers," I know they will.

We may recall in the Bible that Jesus would go off to pray alone. Prayer is mentioned in the Bible one hundred thirty-two times. Even though God was His Father and He may have already known intrinsically what needed to be done, Jesus *still prayed*. Sometimes, He would pray for hours.

Even for Jesus, prayer was a constant in His life, making His soul stronger because His ministry direction was always guided by His Father's advice. Even Jesus, the Son of God, needed prayer to stay connected to His Father. It was His lifeline to peace. He intended to be a role model for us to follow His lead in our earthly lives.

I think we sometimes forget how much Jesus was tempted and persecuted by non-believers. Even His apostles who spent the most time with Him and knew Him best would still challenge Him. They'd ask questions that reflected their weak humanity and difficulty trusting what they witnessed.

I'm sure Jesus got frustrated that His apostles didn't just understand Him by seeing Him in action. They had the opportunity to be with Him every day and see the miracles firsthand, yet they *still* had doubts. I think God, the Father, knew that we *too* would struggle with prayer and blind faith.

Sometimes, I wonder how disillusioned Jesus feels with us today when He ponders all that He endured and how much He suffered on the cross, yet we *still* do not come to Him for guidance.

I wonder how saddened He feels when we are not connecting with Him in prayer, how *He waits for us to reach out and just talk with Him.* He's watching us struggle and reaching out to everyone and anyone but Him. He has given us the gift of scripture to comfort and guide our steps daily.

In John 10:10 we are reminded, "The thief comes only to steal and kill and destroy; I have come that they may have life and live to the full." Jesus waits for us, so He can give us this full life and we sadly forget He's there. We blame Him when prayers aren't answered or when bad things happen, but are we praying to Him regularly with trust, gratitude, and love?

I have to admit that I have not always had this awareness in my life. I too, have asked many people their advice and opinions over the years about personal situations I faced. I resist that urge even today. I know now if I had a more disciplined prayer life in the past, I would have had the answers I sought because I would have had a more intimate relationship with God, my heavenly Father.

In the Old Testament, in the book of Jeremiah 29:11, we hear "For surely I know the plans I have for you, "says the Lord, "plans for your welfare and not for harm, to give you a future with hope."

No one has my back more than God and although the answers I seek may not be as easy as getting a text from a friend, watching a self-help video, or talking for hours on the phone with a trusted advisor, the truth we seek can only come from intimacy with one credible source, our Creator.

Several holy saints and mystics have shared their passion and value they placed on a devoted prayer life. Perhaps one of the greatest mystics of our time was Saint Maria Faustina Kowalska, a Polish nun from the nineteenth century who was canonized on April 30, 2000. She is considered the "Apostle of Mercy" and she left behind her diary, *Divine Mercy in My Soul.*

The legacy of this most holy and devout Polish saint who was only thirty-three years old when she died is that she has provided six inspiring notebooks with almost two thousand entries of her *intimate conversations* with Jesus throughout her life.

The dialogue reflected in her diary is simply one of the most moving exchanges of merciful love, unfailing devotion, and life instruction you'll ever read. Some religious have shared that this might be the second most important book in the world, after the Bible.

You can open it up, start to read at any place in the diary, and be spiritually impacted on a most profound level. Her words written thousands of years ago offer modern-day perspectives that support all of our challenges. Jesus used her as a vehicle of grace that continues to guide any soul-seeking, prayer-filled instruction and direction toward peaceful living.

One of her most illuminating entries highlights *prayer*:

Prayer - a soul arms itself by prayer for all kinds of combat. In whatever state the soul may be, it ought to pray. A soul which is pure and beautiful must pray, or else it will never attain it; a soul which is newly converted must pray, or else it will fall again; a sinful soul, plunged in sins, must pray so that it might rise again. There is no soul which is not bound to pray, for every single grace comes to the soul through prayer. [3]

I reflect over the years when my professional career or family relationships were not going as well as I had hoped, and I did not turn to God. I wish I had read Saint Faustina's diary then. I regret those times and missed real opportunities for enlightenment.

I wasted hours of sharing my angst with others when I could have sought out a quiet place and prayed, listened, and waited for God to guide me. The comfort and advice from well-meaning people, in hindsight, did not solve my problems and oftentimes, that guidance given only provided short-term relief.

In prayerful and prayer-filled moments, I now have started to see that problems and challenges exist and doors close to opportunities because it's simply not God's will for my life at this time. I am accepting of these crosses and I continue to pray. I've let go of my expectations of time and urgency and have let God choose the time needed to let situations resolve themselves. He has never disappointed.

In Mark 7:7, we are encouraged to, "Ask and it will be given to you; seek and you will find; knock and the door will be opened to you." We'd feel at peace if we relied more on scripture as a part of our daily discernment for all our choices and decisions.

Anxiety and fear would not exist to the degree we feel it daily if prayer was a priority. Knowing with confidence that we simply have to be with Him, search for Him, and that He will give us what we need offers extraordinary peace to our soul.

The arrow of the soul that that remains directed and focused on prayer delivers peace to *every quadrant* of the compass. The strongest gravitational pull of temptation, anxiety, and worldly desires will not have any power over one's core and life stability if prayer is a constant in one's life.

When Jesus was asked by His disciples how they should pray, He gave them and us one truly *simple prayer* in the "Our Father". He gave us a way to open our hearts in a very intuitive way, connecting with our Creator in just *seven* sentences.

1. *"Our Father who art in heaven"*:
Recognition that we truly have a Father in heaven who is there for us.

2. *"Hallowed be thy name"*:
Acknowledging that God, Our Father, should be worshipped, praised, and adored.

3. *"Thy kingdom come"*:
There's an eternal plan.

4. *"Thy will be done on earth as it is in heaven"*:
Someone who should be trusted to provide us with His will and plan for our salvation from Earth to heaven.

5. *"Give us this day our daily bread"*:

He will provide for us with daily sustenance through the Eucharist, the living bread of life.

6. *"And forgive us our trespasses as we forgive those that trespass against us"*:
He'll remain merciful to us when we make mistakes as long as we forgive others.

7. *"Lead us not into temptation but deliver us from evil. Amen."*
He will protect us and save us as long as we remain connected to Him.

This prayer takes less than a minute to pray. Can you imagine the impact this *one prayer*, recited daily, could have for strengthening our faith and relationship with God?

If we fervently desire to have a more intimate relationship with God beginning with this *one prayer* each day, we will surely develop a habit of connection. Our good Father *will teach us* how to build on that foundation. We make our lives so much harder by placing high expectations on ourselves. There's no such thing as perfection in prayer. This is an easy gift of peace we can give ourselves generously each day.

Prayer discipline and practice are choices we can easily make that do not require any energy except showing up and having the best intentions. It is helpful however, to choose and create a designated space and establish a time for this in your life as much as you plan out your other daily activities.

Think about the pictures of family members and friends that you have placed in your home that remind you of those that you cherish; *do the same for God.* Make the creation of this space and allocated time a *non-negotiable* item on your to-do list.

Additionally, remember to place your Holy Bible, prayer books, rosaries, and other sacramentals in the car, bedroom, and anywhere in your home or workplace as a visible reminder of the high value you place on them and as a reminder to frequently use them. Adapt your intentions to your lifestyle and make it convenient. The prayerful practices and intentions will follow.

Also, wearing meaningful faith-inspiring jewelry that reflects your devotions will also open up opportunities to strengthen and share your faith with others.

Our society places such a high value on physical fitness. Getting fit spiritually *also* requires the same level of discipline and practice. It requires an emotional commitment to find resources to enhance your personal experience. Physical fitness can be enhanced by equipment but not necessary to be effective. Many exercises simply need the body to engage.

Spiritual fitness *just needs prayer* and an open mind to God's intercession to be impactful and effective. There are so many educational resources and published offerings that are available to us to enhance this practice.

In this way, technology has made it possible to have the convenience of many websites, books, and media platforms that support our prayerful intentions. Sometimes, however, it can be overwhelming and challenging to determine what subscription services and media outlets are the *best of the best*.

Having too many options can also add to the layer of stress that we are trying to avoid. I have been the grateful beneficiary of reading, reviewing, studying, and experimenting with many ideas over the years.

It takes time and commitment to find the right fit for your soul. Be courageous in your search and steadfast in your goals in this quadrant. The evil one will tempt you and persuade you to not believe this is a priority. Do all you can to resist those temptations.

There are numerous excellent recommendations provided in the index. One smartphone application that I use that has been particularly helpful and time-efficient is *Hallow*. It facilitates the consolidation of many *multi-sensory* options for *daily* prayer engagement.

For those that desire a dynamic source for guided prayer, mediation, relaxation, and reflection; *Hallow* presents excellent options and frequent content updates worth exploring.

Having one application that provides scripture readings, prayer access, and opportunities to completely *customize your personality preferences* to your intentions is truly compelling and highly functional. This unique smartphone tool *strengthens the the soul* with modern technological media advances. It is highly recommended.

Resources that facilitate your prayer life are useful, but prayer only requires the *intention and the desire to have intimacy* with God and trusting Him to guide you in the direction that is best for you and you alone. No one can guide you like your Father. He will also guide you to the most valuable resources to enhance your time with Him. Trust Him to always lead.

Making this one change in your daily plans will give you peace and change your life. More so, if you are responsible for others, you will be giving them a valuable gift by encouraging them to follow your lead, also changing *their* lives.

Another powerful prayer you might consider making a priority is the "Holy Rosary". One hundred years ago, the Blessed Mother taught this prayer to three children during her first apparition in Fatima. This singular appearance by the Mother of Jesus delivered a profound message of peace.

Praying the Rosary and meditating on the events of Mary's life with Jesus not only settles our minds to be contemplative but asking for the intercession of Mother and Son during this time carries unprecedented power, healing, and peace. In the last ten years, I have become devoted to praying this prayer every day. This discipline has allowed me to go much deeper in my spirituality.

Our Lady of Fatima promised *peace to the world* when she appeared to those three children in Portugal in 1917. That promise of peace is just as important today as it was in 1917. I feel it abundantly when I pray the Rosary.

In 2010, I was blessed to attend a retreat for Marian Consecration, a devotional practice inspired by Saint Louis de Montfort. This retreat focused on thirty-three days of prayerful devotion to the Sacred Heart of Jesus through the Immaculate Heart of Mary. Praying the Rosary was an integral part of this experience. St. Louis de Montfort, a champion saint of the Rosary, has said, "Never will anyone who says his Rosary every day be led astray. This is a statement I would gladly sign with my blood." [4]

This transformative retreat program has set hundreds of thousands of hearts afire through a parish evangelization program created by Father Michael Gaitley M.I.C. and distributed by the Marians of the Immaculate Conception in Stockbridge, Massachusetts. (See index of resources.)

This *Marian Consecration* Retreat truly changed my spiritual life in just one month. It inspired me to live with a renewed and profound love and appreciation for our Blessed Mother and a clearer understanding of her powerful and intercessory role with her Son.

As children, many of us were keenly aware of her special role in the life of Jesus as His Mother, but as we've gotten older, we have forgotten her influential role in salvation history. Praying the Rosary daily and asking for her intercession became an integral part of the retreat program.

As a young girl, Mary's faith and her "yes" gave us Jesus who became our salvation by dying for our sins, but her motherly support is still available to us today. We can ensure our soul stays on a path to holiness with a devotion and commitment to praying *her* Rosary.

The Rosary, when prayed properly, can be a true life-changing, daily habit that provides an abundance of grace and protection. Saint Louis de Montfort writes, "When the Holy Rosary is said well, it gives Jesus and Mary more glory and is more meritorious than any other prayer." [5]

Meditation on the prayers allows a peaceful walk with our Mother that deepens one's relationship with her, Jesus, and our heavenly Father. The life and death mysteries represent sorrowful, joyful, glorious, and luminous events that connect us to her with greater intimacy.

Imagine in just twenty minutes a day you can do something that has an immediate impact on reducing stress and heightening your awareness of what is truly important. Walking with Mary by meditating on the beads of the rosary through her life mysteries with her Son is as relevant today for our life situations as it was in the Middle Ages.

The Blessed Mother Mary may only be mentioned a few times in the Bible, but her crowning as Queen of Heaven and earthly apparitions that continue today reaffirm her invaluable role in her Son's life and her desire to be our heavenly Mother. Every time she appears to visionaries, she brings the same messages, "Pray the Rosary," "Repent," "Receive the Eucharist," and above all, "Love My Son."

The Rosary is a vehicle of grace that honors our Mother's request, increases our love of Jesus, and gives us a greater awareness of the will of God. It is also the greatest spiritual weapon that has power over Satan. When prayed well and often, the protection of our mother and the company of saints are surely with us, our families, and those we include in our petitions.

There are times when I am approached for advice or asked to listen and support someone who is suffering. I resist the urge to offer a personal opinion and instead ask, "How's your prayer life?" People are surprised by this question because most of us want quick answers and solutions when we are struggling. Many have forgotten the way these simple prayers can bring considerable and consoling power to a soul.

When I've been asked to pray for the sick, dying, and those struggling with depression, anxiety, or substance abuse, I'm quick to explain how their approach to prayer and commitment to that practice has the same power Jesus had when He cured the sick and created miracles.

All of us have the same opportunity each day to teach and encourage those in our circles to put God first in their lives, praying with intensity for their intentions and allowing God to be God. When our prayers are answered, it's equally important that we not forget to tell the story and good news as a way to evangelize and encourage more devotion by other souls.

In life, when we are faced with crisis, pain, and suffering, we are desperate for healing and solutions. Prayer that is only offered for solutions isn't the foundation for a life-fulfilling relationship with our Father.

God is merciful and will still be there for us in our petitions for help, but our peaceful understanding of what is truly best for our soul and those we love comes far more easily when we are actively engaged in an intimate dialogue with God without expectations of the outcome.

Saint Faustina speaks of this intimacy in her diary, *Divine Mercy in My Soul*:

"Neither graces, nor revelations, nor raptures, nor gifts granted to a soul make it perfect, but rather the intimate union of the soul with God. These gifts are mere ornaments of the soul but constitute neither its essence nor its perfection.

My sanctity and perfection consist in the close union of my will with the will of God. God never violates our free will. It is up to us whether we want to receive God's grace or not. It's is up to us whether we will cooperate with it or waste it." [6]

When Jesus rose from the dead three days after His death on the cross, His very first encounter was with a woman in the garden who was weeping. In John 20:15 Jesus asks, "Woman why are you crying?" He did not take away her pain but walked alongside her, comforted her, and gave her a task to go out and bring the good news of His return to the others.

Our mission is the same today.

God knows all of our doubts and fears. He knows it's hard to find those quiet moments to just be in the moment and ask for direction when there are so many influencers in our lives that would just as well give us their opinions.

No one can lead us on the path to peace like the Father. God desires to be our life counselor and consultant. Every good thing will happen as long as we continue to invest time in Him, adoring Him, thanking Him, and seeking His counsel.

When we leave this earthly world and see God, Jesus, the Holy Spirit, the Blessed Mother, and the saints for the first time, it should feel like we are connecting with old friends we've been talking to for years, but just couldn't physically embrace. What a joy that reunion will be!

If you ask someone what it means to be a good friend; one of the qualities would likely include being a good listener and spending time with that person. The best way to listen to God is through His living Word, the Bible. These same qualities hold true for desiring a true friendship with Jesus. We need to dedicate quality time, listen with an open heart, and be mindful of what we hear.

Prayer can't be one-sided, always asking for what we need or think we want. The apostles shared a unique friendship with Jesus as they traveled with him during His ministry. Jesus knew that when He left them, He'd need to send the Holy Spirit to be with them and continue to guide their paths. *This same Spirit is there for us today.* Asking the Holy Spirit to guide our intentions, especially when we might not feel confident in our prayer process, is the best way to ensure you are moving in the right direction.

In the index of this book, you will find a comprehensive listing of prayers to get you started. You will enjoy abundant grace to courageously overcome any obstacles in your path toward holiness and peace as long as you invest time here. Becoming an active member of the *Compass Club* is not possible without a sincere and active commitment to consistent prayer, the fourth quadrant.

COMPASS CONNECTIONS: Reflect on the following scripture passages and write down specific ways you can apply these messages to your plans of making better choices for **Prayer** as part of your new Compass living strategy:

"And when you pray, you must not be like the hypocrites. For they love to stand and pray in the synagogues and at the street corners, that they may be seen by others. Truly, I say to you, they have received their reward. But when you pray, go into your room and shut the door and pray to your Father who is in secret. And your Father who sees in secret will reward you." - Matthew 6: 5-15

_____

_____

_____

_____

"Pray that, according to the riches of his glory, he may grant that you may be strengthened in your inner being with power through his Spirit, and that Christ may dwell in your hearts through faith, as you are being rooted and grounded in love. I pray that you may have the power to comprehend, with all the saints, what is the breadth and length and height and depth, and to know the love of Christ that surpasses knowledge, so that you may be filled with all the fullness of God." - Ephesians 3:16-19

_____

_____

_____

_____

"But the hour is coming, and is now here, when the true worshippers will worship the Father in spirit and truth, for the Father is seeking such people to worship him. God is spirit, and those who worship him must worship in spirit and truth." - John 4:23-24

_____

_____

_____

_____

"But stay awake at all times, praying that you may have strength to escape all these things that are going to take place, and to stand before the Son of Man." - Luke 21:36

_____

_____

_____

_____

COMPASS COMMITMENT: This is what I will personally do to commit to embracing the new ideas in this chapter that will strengthen my soul toward **Prayer** activities that reflect that **Christ is my Core.**

1.

2.

3.

DIRECTING THE ARROW

This week I will commit to daily prayer with a gratitude in my heart as soon as I wake up. I'll stop midday to reflect on my blessings and ask for God's intercession. At bedtime I will reflect on my shortcomings and ask God for the grace to do better the next day. I know that by establishing a habit of praying intentionally each day I will strengthen my soul. This commitment will guide and lead me to knowing God's will for my days and will deepen my relationship with Him. (see index of recommended prayers)

Bonus: I will learn or revisit how to pray the Rosary by using a guided application on my phone or a prayer booklet that will offer reflections to help me truly *pray* the mysteries. I will commit to twenty minutes each day praying the Rosary for one week.

JOURNAL REFLECTIONS FOR THE WEEK:

_____
_____
_____
_____
_____
_____
_____
_____
_____
_____
_____
_____
_____
_____
_____
_____
_____
_____
_____
_____
_____
_____
_____
_____

CHAPTER 5:

ALMSGIVING AND ADORATION: IT IS GIVING THAT WE RECEIVE

John: 13: 13-15

"You call me "teacher" and "master" and rightly so indeed I am. If I, therefore, the master and teacher, have washed your feet, you ought to wash one another's feed. I have given you a model to follow, so that as I have done for you, you should also do."

As Christians, we are called to serve and encouraged to perform regular acts of charity, especially toward the poor, marginalized, and less fortunate. A disciplined life that embraces almsgiving or giving charitably as a way to *live intentionally* and *consistently* each day will find peace, joy, and have a renewed sense of life purpose.

Almsgiving with a *Compass Club* mentality is never an afterthought but a *mindset* to invest time here purposefully and daily. A soul directed toward this quadrant creates a path to peace for all. In the Bible, there are *twenty-nine references* to almsgiving that reaffirm the vital importance that Jesus placed on this activity for the soul. We should give for the love of other souls, not for any personal benefit or reward.

Jesus speaks of this when He spoke to his apostles in Matthew 6: 1-18:

> Take care not to perform righteous deeds in order that people may see them; otherwise, you will have no recompense from your heavenly Father. When you give alms do not blow a trumpet before you, as the hypocrites do in the synagogues and the streets to win the praise of others.

Amen, I say to you, they have received their reward. But when you do give alms, do not let your left hand know what your right is doing, so that your almsgiving may be in secret. And your Father who sees in secret will repay you.

Today, we live in a world that celebrates success by getting ahead. The acquisition of material goods is a sign and symbol of true success in life. We desire this success and financial stability, yet once goals are achieved, many of us can still feel unhappy and unsatisfied.

Charitable activities and outreach efforts can be seen throughout our vast communities, but too often this happens as an *afterthought* or something we only do when asked. For many, we give charitably when we've *first* taken care of our own needs comfortably.

Pandemics, natural disasters, and fluctuating financial markets create chaos. Fear of not having what we need drives many tough decisions for our families. Many people today, unfortunately, wait until they are economically stable before they can justify being charitable to others on any regular basis.

It's hard to argue with this worldly rationale when many of us fear not being able to provide for ourselves and our families. Living here on Earth is our reality. The promise of eternal life isn't something we are guaranteed. We do live in unpredictable and uncertain financial times.

There might be books out there that heaven is a real place, but some remain skeptical. Focusing on what we can see *here and now* seems to be the best way to live our lives. The world tells us to safeguard our treasures while financial markets are unsteady and job security is not guaranteed. *God sees things differently.*

The *Compass Club* mentality sees this quadrant differently as well. Almsgiving is an *intentional activity* that *doesn't wait for comfort* before giving of ourselves for others.

We are reminded especially during the Lenten season that prayer, fasting, and almsgiving are the three pillars or practices most pleasing to God. Sadly, giving freely without reciprocal benefits is not always the way of our world.

By nature, I do believe most of us truly have an innate desire to help others and many do what they can when called upon to serve, but we could be doing much more, *more often*. When our soul consistently moves in this direction without ensuring our own security *first*, we will experience inner peace that positively impacts every other area of our life.

In 2020, our world became paralyzed by the COVID-19 virus pandemic. Many were crippled with extraordinary financial loss, were unable to do anything but survive, and make hard choices for their own families. Millions of people are still out of work and thousands of small businesses did not survive. It will likely take a decade or longer for many to recover from the unprecedented losses.

There are countless charitable and selfless stories of people giving back to others that fill our hearts with hope and joy amid such loss of life and fear of the unknown during times like these. Nothing feeds our hearts and souls with happiness more than being a beacon of light and hope for someone who needs us. Not everyone who gave had a surplus. That's the *Compass Club* way of understanding almsgiving.

We hear so many uplifting stories of selfless love that inspire us with hope, but do we take proactive action? Understandably, not everyone can be a leader of initiatives to give back to those less fortunate, but a soul that is sensitive to the needs of others will respond often to support *anyone put in their path regardless of their financial comfortability*. Giving back doesn't always involve monetary donations.

The Prayer of St. Francis of Assisi often associated with the popular song "Make Me a Channel of Your Peace" reminds us "it is in giving that we receive."[7]

When we allow ourselves to be a channel of God's peace, we give more, we receive more grace, and can do more. Christ fills the soul with unfathomable grace and the resources needed to act.

We must invite God often into this intention for our soul. Investing our time and moving in the direction of almsgiving as a *regular, daily practice* is a sure way to strengthen our core because the love of Christ will guide us to be our most giving selves.

The healthy balance of our compass lives can be more greatly achieved when we are giving of ourselves to others with greater intentional purpose. The peace of Christ will flow from our hearts to the souls of those that need us the most and all of those involved will be transformed.

I've always appreciated the story of Jesus at the Last Supper as a story packed with rich lessons for life direction. The story of His departure from His earthly life was sad, but it was His decision to wash the feet of His apostles that had the greatest impact on my heart. During his very *last time* with them, He knelt to be *charitable*, humbling himself to wash their dirty feet.

In those days, the people of that time walked for days. They were lacking in the conveniences of our time without cell phones and cars to travel and make connections. Some trips took days to reach their final destination and they were certainly not traveling in heavily cushioned sneakers.

They wore sandals everywhere and their feet were probably the dirtiest part of their bodies. Our humble master and teacher, Jesus, chose to wash their feet as a grand gesture of love and service. This act of love was intended to teach the apostles and us what Jesus expected, *that we do this for others*.

Almsgiving doesn't have to be a grand gesture or a big check. We can invite God into these decisions and petition Him in daily prayer to put us on the path with someone or something that needs our attention. *He will act in us.* We let God know that we truly desire to give alms and be the feet, hands, eyes, and ears of Jesus to be a light for others.

We must remain open to where that leads us because sometimes, it will not be convenient, and we may need to get our hands dirty and possibly wash some feet.

Our world is in such grave need right now and will continue to face economic hardships. Everywhere we turn, it appears that there are such extreme needs and unfathomable poverty. We see so many families and communities who are struggling just to put food on the table.

In addition to physical poverty, many are emotionally impoverished and simply need companionship and someone to give time to listen, support, and offer hope. It's hard to decide where to invest the most time and resources because it appears hopeless at times that our giving is having any significant impact.

As we navigate uncharted waters, we sometimes rely on our instincts regarding decisions to help. Again, this is where an intimate friendship with Jesus paves the way toward *precision in our purpose.*

Any decision we make to use our free will to help others is highly esteemed from above. In Galatians 5:13 we are reminded, "You my brothers and sisters were called to be free but do not use your freedom to indulge the flesh; rather, serve one another humbly in love."

The temptation might be to hold on to what resources we do have for fear that we might not be able to provide for ourselves long term. *God can and will lead us in this area.* I have had so many opportunities unveiled to me over the years to reach out to impoverished and spiritually lonely souls.

I know that in many situations, these ideas simply did not come from my mind or intellect, God was driving the ideas. I gave Him my "yes" to serve and the opportunities were abundant. I know these circumstances were divinely ordered. Not only did God allow me to serve, but I was changed for the better too.

Jeremiah 29:11 reminds us that, "For I know the plans I have for you, plans to give you hope and a future." We simply have to cooperate and trust.

Sometimes the need is simply a phone call to an elderly neighbor, a letter to a soldier, or an anonymous meal for a struggling family. It might be just letting someone in line in front of you at the supermarket who has a few items. A smile to someone who is scowling at us in traffic is an act of charitable intent. That one act of kindness could open up doors to their souls that only the Holy Spirit can, but He needs our attention and active participation to work the miracles.

Almsgiving comes from the heart and there's never anything that comes with pure intentions to give to another that isn't a perfect gift. When one's compass reflects the light that comes from a generous heart and soul, everyone on that path is illuminated and lifted higher. By focusing our heart-felt intentions on this quadrant of our compass, we will be filling our soul with beautiful energy for the journey back to heaven.

Our intention to be the one to wash another's feet will evangelize others and reflect the lessons Jesus taught His apostles at that Last Supper many years ago. Following the Lord who was the consummate example of charitable love will always lead to light.

John's Gospel 8:12 reminds us, "I am the light of the world, whoever follows me will not walk in darkness but will have the light of life". This light of life is not just geared toward heaven.

Living in light brings hope and that emotion leads to peace here and now. Nothing fills a heart with more joy than knowing you had a positive impact on someone's life, especially when they were walking in darkness.

We can have the best intentions of following God and staying in the light, but it's really hard to know *where* to focus your time, talents, and energy on any given day. How can anyone really know where God wants you? How do we know where to invest our time for the greatest good?

Jesus shed some light on this dilemma when He prayed and *fasted* in the desert. He went there to discern how His Father wanted Him to serve during His earthly ministry. Historically, almsgiving has always been a term we heard most predominately tied to *prayer and fasting* during the Lenten season, a sacred time of forty days to focus our hearts and minds on God.

It's a time to walk spiritually as Jesus did for those forty days leading up to His passion, death, and resurrection. Those forty days in the desert were a time of fasting and prayer for Jesus, but also a time of great temptation.

During those times of great human and physical weakness, He was challenged by Satan but, it was His reliance on his Father's Word and the power of the Holy Spirit that enabled *His soul to be enlightened during that fasting period.*

He was directed more clearly to His three-year ministry and mission that began shortly thereafter. This same practice of fasting can also have a similar impact on your intention to know where and how to serve others.

Embracing the idea of fasting beyond Lent on a more regular basis is a way to go spiritually deeper in your prayer life and to follow our Lord's example in that desert. Fasts do not have to be for forty days, but the intention behind your sacrifice, for any amount of time, is profoundly valued by God. Denying your body of food, sweets, and other delights has strengthened my soul during these times.

Sometimes, a fast isn't about deprivation of the body. Fasting can also be eliminating anything that causes you to be sinful. There are hundreds of books about the practice of fasting and countless saints who extol the virtues of this practice, but it is only in *committing to this practice* that the blessings unfold. Fasting creates a path for life transformation.

Fasting is a way to not just give up what you enjoy most but to experience a poverty of spirit that inspires you to let God work in you more completely. Its purpose in the most grace-filled way is to give up what is pleasing to you so that you can remain more centered on prayer and connection to Him as well as know *where you are most needed to serve.*

When you wonder how to truly *know where God wants you to serve,* fasting is a discipline that allows you to empty your reserves and allow God's grace to fill you back up in the most perfect way. You are inviting Him to fill you up according to His will.

Nothing I've done in my life to date has given me greater divine insights and spiritual growth than when I sacrifice in this way. The ability to strengthen and direct the arrow of one's soul in light of the questions of *where and how to serve* is manifested greatly through the practice of *fasting.*

That intimacy of your soul united with Christ is supercharged. *Fasting, prayer, and almsgiving* are indeed a three-fold gift you can offer to the Holy Trinity: Father, Son, and Holy Spirit.

One of my favorite authors on this subject is Father Slavko Barbanic, O.F.M. in his book, *Fasting.* He believed that "fasting was the soul of prayer":

> Fasting and prayer are not ends in themselves, but only means to recognize and to accept the will of God, and to solicit the grace of perseverance in carrying it out in being open to God's plan, and in walking in the footsteps of Christ.
>
> Peace is something dynamic; it cannot be bought or sold. It prospers only in the hearts of people who are capable of forgiving and of loving those who have wronged and hurt them.
>
> Fasting is a prayer of the whole body; it is prayer through the body. Fasting shows that our body must participate in our prayer, and that our prayer must become carnal in order to be prayer in the fullest sense of the word. [8]

The call to serve will continue to be demanding. Many today are as hungry for peace as they are for physical resources. The global pandemic of 2020 didn't just cause suffering and loss of life, but many people are still feeling fearful and lack hope for a promising future.

By nature, we feel compassion and love for others but also can feel paralyzed by the task. There are so many distractions and for many of us, we have just enough energy to take care of our own families. "What can we do? How much can we do? When can we jump in to serve?" are difficult questions many families are asking.

Be encouraged that the almsgiving you desire will be made possible with greater clarity *when you pray and fast*. No act of pure service, no matter how small, will have an imperfect impact.

Be comforted that the will of God will prevail when you lead your soul toward the *intention of giving back* to others. God will guide you toward His perfect will for your life and He will make the connections needed for your soul and those that need you most.

Another spiritual resource that can offer greater clarity in these matters of the heart is a unique Catholic practice of spending time in *adoration*. This devotional activity has also had a significant and profound impact on my charitable outreach efforts. This daily and weekly investment of my time has given me the *"light of life"* that John speaks of in chapter eight.

For those of us raised as *cradle* Catholics, the practice of adoration or *spending time in front of the blessed Eucharist* in a chapel was not something we did or even understood. It simply wasn't highlighted as part of my formation in the church traditions.

Adoration is going to church and spending a *holy hour* with the Lord outside of your regular church visits. The consecrated and blessed host is placed in a monstrance that is placed on the altar where you sit quietly and adore Jesus. You can pray the Rosary, read from the Bible, meditate on books written by saints, or just sit in silence and listen to what comes to your mind, heart, and soul.

Here you will find peace and a welcome relief from the noise of the outside world. Investing time here will enhance your friendship with Jesus. You are essentially choosing to give your free time to God without any obligations that are required. It's a gift to Him in the purest sense.

This is a divinely inspired way to get answers to your pressing questions. This is a place where the arrow of my soul has been greatly strengthened; not just relative to the important question of *where to serve* but in every quadrant of my compass. God's plans for my soul are always made clearer after time spent in adoration.

During adoration, you are affirming your devotion to and worship of Jesus who you believe is present in body, blood, soul, and divinity under the appearance of the consecrated host or the sacramental bread. It would make perfect sense you'd go to visit Jesus where He is if you desire an authentic friendship with Him. Fortunately, I've matured in my understanding of what a real relationship with God feels like and have augmented my prayer life by more frequent adoration visits in a chapel.

My insights about my life direction have become so much clearer the more time I invest in quiet time away from the distractions of my day and the expectations others have of me while I'm in a chapel praying and adoring God. The peace that flows from my soul is so profound; I simply must come back over and over again for more.

This is why *adoration and almsgiving* go hand in hand in our *Compass Club* lifestyle plans. We were not created to be selfish beings. We were created to serve others and build up the body of Christ, but we can't expect to know what God wants of us unless we spend time with Him without the distractions of our world.

When we visit Jesus and worship Him in the form of the Eucharist outside of mass, we are honoring and comforting His Sacred Heart. This brings Him such joy because He waits for us there.

Many saints have written beautiful reflections from their experiences in adoration but one that is most noteworthy is a sixteenth-century mystic, Saint Margaret Mary Alacoquo, is best known for her true devotion to the Sacred Heart of Jesus.

During revelations, she received by the Lord she was asked to spend a *Holy Hour* before the Blessed Sacrament.
Jesus told her, "I have a burning thirst to be honored by men in the Blessed Sacrament." [9]

The Catechism of the Catholic Church further explains:

> Adoration is the first attitude of man acknowledging that he is a creature before his Creator. It exalts the greatness of the Lord who made us and the almighty power of the

Savior who sets us free from evil. Adoration is homage of the spirit to the "King of Glory," respectful silence in the presence of the "ever greater" God. Adoration of the thrice-holy and sovereign God of love blends with humility and gives assurance to our supplications. [10]

In Matthew 11:28 Jesus said, "Come to me all who are weary and find life burdensome and I will refresh you." This scripture verse encapsulates what I know to be true about the practice of adoration. I go into the chapel feeling overwhelmed, tired, and filled with questions and I leave there in a state of peace and well-being in the core of my soul.

When the arrow of your soul is directed there, you will know exactly *where you must go* and *how you can be your best self for others* who need you. Adoration allows me time to sit with the only friend who truly knows my soul.

There are several great resources published about adoration. Many saints have spoken of the how and the why, but it's only in *doing it* that you will see first-hand the blessings that come from participating.

Saint Mother Teresa of Calcutta, one of the most well-known saints of our time, also strongly encouraged adoration practice and attributed many of the blessings she received for her *charitable causes* and global impact helping the poor to the time she invested here.

In the book, *Praying with Mother Teresa*, we are inspired by her words of advice:

Nowhere on earth are you more welcomed, nowhere on earth are you more loved, than by Jesus living and truly present in the Most Blessed Sacrament. The time you spend with Jesus in the Blessed Sacrament is the best time that you will spend on earth.

Each moment that you spend with Jesus will deepen your union with Him and make your soul everlastingly more glorious and beautiful in Heaven and will help bring about an everlasting peace on earth. [11]

I have intentionally set a goal of spending time with our Lord, each day in adoration, and have had remarkable and mystical experiences that have provided years of insight into my past and my plans for the future. Visiting for fifteen minutes or one hour is not as important as your pure intention to simply go there.

During this time, I take notes about the thoughts I have and how I imagine Jesus speaking to me. I offer my heartfelt gratitude each time. Just being still with God is a blessing everyone should experience. There's no prescribed way to go to adoration.

Just go and be still.

God knows what you need. Think of adoration as professional spiritual development and continuing education in as much as you'd attend a class to perfect your trade or business.

The illuminated path that shines brightly from time spent in adoration is real. Your spiritual vision becomes clearer and a true sense of peace abounds. It is an intentional and purposeful living strategy for peace. It is true that for the practices of almsgiving and adoration that *what you give is what you will receive*: bountiful grace, insights, and peace.

Giving back to others and giving back to our Creator is a key component of strengthening your soul and keeping your core strong, focusing on the best path for your life and those entrusted to your care.

Lastly, when we take the time and sacrifice other things by choosing instead to be with Jesus in the Blessed Sacrament through faith in what cannot be seen, we give great comfort to our Him. We console His heart who thirsts for our companionship.

In the silence of that chapel, I feel a connection that is intimate and sacred. This singular practice truly refreshes my soul and quiets my mind. Adoration allows me to escape the demands of living in a busy world and to just focus on being quiet and peaceful at the moment.

I am reminded that I was created for a divine purpose and even when I am faced with self-doubt; my Lord raises me up. He gives me confidence and I proceed with steadfast confidence that He is walking alongside me to the path that is His will and not one driven by my ego.

Be comforted by these words in John 16:33, "I have told you these things so that in me you will have peace." This investment of time on any given day will direct your soul in the most enlightening and peaceful way.

COMPASS CONNECTIONS: Reflect on the following scripture passages and write down specific ways you can apply these messages to your plans of making better choices for **Almsgiving** in your new Compass Club living strategy:

"And the King will answer them, 'Truly, I say to you, as you did it to one of the least of these my brothers, you did it to me.'" - Matthew 25:40

_____
_____
_____
_____

"Beware of practicing your righteousness before men to be noticed by them; otherwise you have no reward with your Father who is in heaven. "So, when you give to the poor, do not sound a trumpet before you, as the hypocrites do in the synagogues and in the streets, so that they may be honored by men." - 2 Corinthians 9:6

_____
_____
_____
_____

"Sell your possessions and give to the poor. Provide purses for yourselves that will not wear out, a treasure in heaven that will never fail, where no thief comes near and no moth destroys. For where your treasure is, there your heart will be also." - Luke 12:33

_____
_____
_____
_____

"What good is it, my brothers, if someone says he has faith but does not have works? Can that faith save him? If a brother or sister is poorly clothed and lacking in daily food, and one of you says to them, "Go in peace, be warmed and filled," without giving them the things needed for the body, what good is that? So also, faith by itself, if it does not have works, is dead." - James 2:14-17

_____
_____
_____
_____

COMPASS COMMITMENT: This is what I will personally do to commit to embracing the new ideas in this chapter that will strengthen my soul toward **Almsgiving** activities that reflect that **Christ is my Core.**

1.

2.

3.

DIRECTING THE ARROW

This week I will reach out to a charitable cause or impoverished community and contribute in a meaningful way. I remain open to any inspiration that I receive during Adoration and will go where God sends me even if it's not convenient. I will invest time to share my gifts to improve the lives of another. If possible, I will make a long-term commitment to be an active presence in this community or for this worthy cause.

COMPASS CONNECTIONS: Reflect on the following scripture passages and write down specific ways you can apply these messages to your plans of making better choices for **Adoration** in your new Compass Club living strategy:

"But as for me, by Your abundant loving kindness I will enter Your house, At Your holy temple I will bow in reverence for You." - Psalm 5:7

_____

_____

_____

_____

"Seek the Lord and his strength; seek his presence continually!" - 1 Chronicles 16:11

_____

_____

_____

_____

"But I, through the abundance of your steadfast love, will enter your house. I will bow down toward your holy temple in the fear of you." - Psalm 5:7

_____

_____

_____

_____

"If you abide in me, and my words abide in you, ask whatever you wish, and it will be done for you. By this my Father is glorified, that you bear much fruit and so prove to be my disciples." - John 15:7-8

_____
_____
_____
_____

"Abbey Fest" Adoration, Daylesford Abbey, Paoli PA September 2017

COMPASS COMMITMENT: This is what I will personally do to commit to embracing the new ideas in this chapter that will strengthen my soul toward **Adoration** activities that support **Christ is my Core.**

1.

2.

3.

DIRECTING THE ARROW

This week I will research the Adoration hours my church offers, or I will find another Church that has perpetual adoration. I will commit to at least *one hour* to be with God in this sacred place. I will promise to do this *once a week* to keep the arrow of my soul strongest and directed where God wants to lead. I will bring a journal or notebook with me to record what insights God shares with me during this holy hour.

JOURNAL REFLECTIONS FOR THE WEEK:

_____

_____

_____

_____

_____

_____

_____

_____

_____

_____

_____

_____

_____

_____

_____

_____

_____

_____

_____

_____

_____

CHAPTER 6:

SCRIPTURE: THE SOUL STRENGTHENING TOOL

2 Timothy 3:16-17

"All Scripture is breathed out by God and profitable for teaching, for reproof, for correction, and for training in righteousness, that the man of God may be competent, equipped for every good work."

You've probably heard that the Bible is often called the "living Word of God", yet this masterpiece remains untouched by many of us as a tried and true resource for living our best lives. I've been equally at fault here my entire life.

We instead rely upon easier and more convenient access to popular media, books, magazines, blogs, Ted Talks, YouTube videos, and other *visual* resources to get the life guidance we need. Our Bibles often remain on a bookshelf collecting dust.

Our minds and bodies are still not at peace despite the plethora of content options available to us twenty-four hours a day, seven days a week. The internet offers so many digital content opportunities that we fail to recognize and respect the Bible and scripture as the *life guide* it was written to be.

We are impatient beings and very busy seeking out the best advice and wisdom from popular sources, peer validated, and easier to interpret. Summer book clubs will opt for what's trendy and light-hearted.

The Bible isn't something we consider to be a resource for today's current issues. The *strongest* soul is one that points to scripture consistently as an *intentional* activity versus an afterthought.

Reading scripture for life's most pressing problems feeds the soul in powerful ways. It's the only book that truly reflects the heart of God's intentions for us. Those that support a *Compass Club* life mentality value this resource above all others and actively seek the wisdom that flows from its pages.

As a child growing up Catholic, I was required to memorize the *Baltimore Catechism*, a book of rules and sacramental guidelines that I was expected to learn as a student of the faith. Scripture was only something I heard at Mass on Sundays and even then, what was spoken at the pulpit did not always reflect a clear understanding of the readings. Some priests were better than others for making real-world applications, but most of the time the living Word felt dead to me.

As I matured in my faith, I started to have a deeper curiosity for the Bible but continued to feel overwhelmed by it. The Old Testament felt irrelevant to my world and even though the New Testament felt a bit more relatable, I was uninspired and impatient to read and reflect. Again, I felt obligated to read it, but not necessarily as a guide to my life.

It is in the last decade that I began to understand that taking quiet time to read, reflect, and react to the true meaning of the scriptural passages in the Bible had real power. I began to pray more to the Holy Spirit for guidance in finding what my soul needed.

I made more connections from my head to my heart because the pressure was off for me to interpret it alone. Investing more time with this resource changed my relationship with God and my life changed dramatically. The wisdom that came to me through scriptural reflections delivered such peace to my soul.

Today, we ask Siri, Alexa, and Google to find all the answers to our most pressing questions instead of going to God first. We use GPS for driving instructions and search engines like Google, so we can get whatever information we need to know in seconds.

We have newer technologies like Waze that even anticipate the roadblocks and delays we can anticipate in traffic. Various sites push out *their* recommended connections, friends, and events that match our profiles and the technology conveniently maps content to our preferences.

Have you noticed that you can't even write an electronic letter these days without the auto-correct finishing our sentences? Our ability and intention to think, analyze, and problem solve are being replaced by technologies that rob us of our true feelings and predispositions. We love the conveniences of our technological amenities to get answers and go where we need to go, but at what cost to our soul's identity and intimacy with our Creator?

Scripture is just as accessible as social media resources but reflecting on what God wants to share with us takes *time, planning,* and a *sincere desire* to develop a more intimate relationship with Him. No one can teach and guide you better than your Creator through His life-giving words.

This can be a habit that is formed now and will have a far greater impact on your long-term happiness and peace-filled dispositions than any investment in technology or social media. Trusting this process is necessary to remain on a path that leads to peace and joyful living.

Getting to know God is the surest path to knowing ourselves. Reading scripture and going to the Bible for answers is like going to a new fitness class or trying a new exercise activity. Muscles are stretched and sometimes body movements need practice and adjustments before it becomes second nature. Spiritual fitness needs our time and attention if we want balance and peace.

The living Word of scripture with the intercessory power of the Holy Spirit will touch your soul and offer a level of support and guidance to all of your life decisions that will be transformative.

When you are investing time here and sharing your insights with others who support your soul, you will be part of a community that offers real intimacy and more soulful connections.

Your mind and heart will be directed in much healthier ways if you replaced just *thirty minutes* a day reading the Bible that you'd otherwise spend on your devices accessing the internet or social media each day.

There are numerous smartphone applications for the Bible that make daily access *very convenient* and provide seamless integration into our busy lifestyles. Some websites push content to our computers and phones that deliver daily meditations, mass readings, and even daily Bible verses for private reflections. The index lists many recommendations to review and consider.

God intentionally designed us to be *in communion with Him and each other* to build up the Body of Christ but He did not intend for us to forget about His Word. It does make sense that we are intrinsically drawn to anything that invites us to feel validated, comforted, and part of a community of like-minded individuals and receive instant gratification. Unfortunately, an arrow pointed to social media consistently will never give us the communion our soul needs to thrive.

By nature, we gravitate toward those that share our views and values, but we also are emotionally and spiritually affected by those that don't share our beliefs, values, and intentions on social media platforms. We connect without limitations or filters to those things we probably should not see that can lead us to a false sense of well-being.

We are investing inordinate amounts of time posting images and messages that may not even represent our true feelings and intentions. The living Word of God always offers *pure* content that enhances one's well-being in ways *no other resource* can provide. If we are being honest with ourselves, we know that social media does not intrinsically bring peace to our hearts.

Sometimes, we hesitate to post our honest opinions knowing that we won't be *liked* or worse, we will be publicly rejected. People we don't even know well are directing our attachments to their approval. Our authentic selves are typically not being reflected in what we share. This is not peaceful activity.

Social media may offer instant connectivity, but this addictive interactivity doesn't offer emotional peace. Social media can be a good resource when used wisely, but *never* at the exclusion of time spent with scripture.

Making a firm decision to allocate quiet time to pray and reflect on the Word of God creates limitless opportunities for contentment. That validation will come only when we sit in silence. This may be a new behavior for us to consider, but it's surely a path toward peace. *We need this solitude.* Our souls crave this intimacy. We need to think for ourselves and listen to what our Creator is saying.

In Proverbs 19:21 we are also told that, "Many are the plans in a man's heart, but it is the Lord's purpose that prevails." There are thousands of passages in the Bible that were written to comfort and guide us; offering hope and purpose, yet many of us will never know them because we have not taken the time to patiently explore the depth of this resource.

You will feel deeply connected to God when you make a commitment to spiritual exploration with scripture. The Bible gives you unlimited access and advice from the world's holiest minds.

Throughout John's gospels, Jesus encouraged His followers to remain in His Word and they'd receive truth and clarity. Today, He promises us *freedom* in that pursuit of truth as His cherished disciples. Many of the answers we seek are as close as picking up the Bible and quietly reflecting on what God has to say.

I see now that most of my adult life I was seeking truth all too often from people, places, and things that did not know my soul or the path I was supposed to follow. These advisors had the best of intentions but, they were not God.

Many Christian friends who have always used the Bible as their life guide gave me the following guidelines during my own journey:

1. Create a sacred space in your home.

2. Set a designated time and a firm commitment daily as part of a regular appointment with yourself.

3. Make this practice non-negotiable.

4. Be prayerful and patient.

5. Journal what you hear and what you are feeling as you reflect as this can yield profound insights you might forget.

At first, my thoughts were unorganized but the more diligent I was about keeping a schedule that included this time for God, the easier those ideas and thoughts were managed. These mentors inspired me to invest time in this quadrant *every day* as they did. Countless blessings and surprising insights unfolded for me. This practice has become a non-negotiable plan for my life.

When I'm investing more time reading scripture, I can face conflict, self-doubt, and any challenging situation with greater confidence and clarity. The living Word of God does *breathe life* into my life decisions.

My mind is more often at peace these days because of this simple change I've made by reading scripture as a top priority. I'm off balance when I miss just one day using this resource. It's a practice that offers abundant grace and powerful insights that allow us to lead our most purposeful lives.

Parents and caretakers that live this way are giving their children such a great legacy of witnessing the power of strong faith traditions. A parent who spends quiet time in prayer and reading from the Bible sends a strong message to their children and impacts their relationships in truly positive ways.

A child will make an even stronger commitment to pray themselves when they see their parents praying together. There's no other comprehensive resource that can offer insights and direction like the Bible.

The internet provides so many opportunities for self-improvement. We are also inundated daily with talk shows and news broadcasts that recommend movies, books, and other entertainment options on popular streaming services and specialty channels. It can be overwhelming and stressful to consider where to invest our energy if and when we do have free time to spare.

These other outlets can be very entertaining but, if we invest time in these secular social channels, we should also allow *equal time* for spiritual development to strike a healthy balance of mind, body, and soul. The Bible, in *just one book,* gives access to a variety of genres, authors, life guidance, and mentorship that is a profound way to connect with God.

There is freedom in scripture study because there are no rules or expectations. Self-study options, Bible study groups, and online applications can feed us scripture daily. Reading the Bible should be an integral goal of daily exploration and application to your life.

God will speak to you at first in a whisper, but He will guide you when you fully open your heart to His Word and His truth. You have to simply open it. Just having the intention in your heart to know God on a deeper level through His Word will afford you the opportunities and the grace to take the first steps. Find your Bible today, dust it off, place it in clear view in your home, and ask God to direct your soul.

I've had many situations over the years where God directed me in unimaginable ways once I made Scripture a life priority. Sometimes He makes His intentions for my soul known in unexpected places.

I was about to begin writing this particular chapter on scripture and feeling somewhat insecure. As a novice student of the Bible, I was still learning and developing. I lacked confidence that I could give this quadrant the full credibility it deserved.

To make matters even worse, I was rejected by someone who questioned my plans to even write the book. They asked, "Who are you to write such a book?" "What you are writing about isn't anything new, it can be found in plenty of books."

I was deflated, to say the least. I wanted to stop writing. Rejection is never easy.

I was immediately directed to my Bible and reread a few Gospel accounts on rejection found in Matthew 20:19, Mark 10:34, and Luke 18:32. These passages described how our Lord was mocked, persecuted and rejected during His passion. I immediately felt comforted.

I also opened my Bible to the Book of Psalms 17:1-15 and felt strengthened by this reflection on persecution:

> I call upon you; answer me, O God, turn your ear to me; hear my prayer. Show your wonderful love, you who deliver with your right arm those who seek refuge from their foes. Keep me as the apple of your eye; hide me in the shadow of your wings from the violence of the wicked. My ravenous enemies press upon me, they close their hearts, they fill their mouths with proud roaring. Their steps even now encircle me; they watch closely, keeping low to the ground. Rise, O Lord, confront and cast them down; rescue me from the wicked. I am just-let me see your face; when I awake, let me be filled with your presence.

My mind and spirit drifted off to thoughts of the life of the Blessed Mother and the great suffering she experienced as reflected in the sorrowful mysteries. Her walk with Her Son as He suffered was anything but easy. She watched Him flogged and beaten senselessly and then crowned with thorns. I still felt wounded, but I continued to pray for guidance and affirmation from the Holy Spirit. I did not phone a friend but went to the Bible instead.

I was able to draw some strength from praying to our Blessed Mother in that moment. I decided to keep writing and praying for a direction to see what might transpire. I would have remained depressed, disillusioned, and unproductive without the words of scripture comforting me. *I may have given up.*

No sooner had this incident happened when I needed to take my daughter to the Department of Motor Vehicles for her permit test. I was still feeling disillusioned. My spirit was hurting. It was then and there that I had a most unexpected spiritual encounter with another mother who was also waiting for her son to take his permit test for the *second* time.

Her son was standing behind my daughter in a long line of at least thirty people. I introduced myself and he introduced me to his mom. Of all the people my daughter might have been near in this very, very long line, this young man's mother not only was a Christian, but she was also an author of several bible studies for women.

We had almost two hours to talk about her family, her ministry and her inspiration to write eleven books! She also felt the same self-doubt mostly due to the fact that she had no prior training as an author at the beginning of her call to write. She shared her personal story and I was inspired to continue writing.

She was placed in my path at the *exact time and day* that I was beginning to write this chapter. She advised me to continue to pray and if it was truly God's will, He would provide the words and show me the path as He had done for her. She shared her feelings of insecurity relative to her qualifications to write. She encouraged me to have faith and trust Him as she had done. She advised me to be patient and pray. How timely was that encounter?

Some may think that perhaps this was just a coincidence that her son was behind my daughter in line and his mom was sitting in her car just two cars away from mine in a busy parking lot. What if I never said hello to her son? That voice in my head prompting me was an answer to a prayer. Relying on scripture that day lifted my spirits and moved me in the direction God wanted me.

That morning, I was praying fervently for direction and needed confirmation that this book was still God's intention. I brought my computer and Bible to do my work while I waited for my daughter's test to be finished. I brought these items with me, but my mind was still conflicted.

Above all, God knew that this chapter would be my hardest to write and He knew that I was the least confident in this quadrant.

The Holy Spirit truly showed up for me on that day and I left feeling quite peaceful. That day, none of us believed that we were not supposed to meet. This spiritual encounter completely affirmed for me that God knew my heart was troubled and He sent an angel to lift me up. God has a plan for our lives, especially for those that remain loyal to Him.

Sharing our faith to strengthen our soul for good purposes and leaning on God often creates miraculous opportunities to meet beautiful souls that will enlighten us and move us along in the direction of our most purposeful lives.

Fear, rejection, and suffering are a reality in our world, but God's Word truly is a *living source* of comfort to anyone who chooses to openly welcome Him into their everyday life decisions and events. Later that afternoon, I received a text from her saying, "We would never have met if my son had passed his test the first time. God is so good!"

This story is shared so that you will be inspired to seek the many divinely inspired opportunities available to you and to remain open to those whispers. *Scripture clears the path to peace.* The power of this living Word will breathe new life into all of your plans, known and unknown.

You simply have to exercise your free will and invite God into your life decisions. Scripture is *the* strengthening tool for your soul. It has the power to direct our actions in only those ways that reflect God's perfect will for our lives. Choose this quadrant often and be transformed.

COMPASS CONNECTIONS: Reflect on the following scripture passages and write down specific ways you can apply these bible messages to your **Scripture** practice as part of your new Compass living strategy:

"The seed falling among the thorns refers to someone who hears the word, but the worries of this life and the deceitfulness of wealth choke the word, making it unfruitful. But the seed falling on good soil refers to someone who hears the word and understands it. This is the one who produces a crop, yielding a hundred, sixty or thirty times what was sown." - Matthew 13:19-23

_____

_____

_____

_____

"Let the word of Christ dwell in you richly, teaching and admonishing one another in all wisdom, singing psalms and hymns and spiritual songs, with thankfulness in your hearts to God." - Colossians 3:16

_____

_____

_____

_____

"For the word of God is living and active, sharper than any two-edged sword, piercing to the division of soul and of spirit, of joints and of marrow, and discerning the thoughts and intentions of the heart." - Hebrews 4:12

_____
_____
_____
_____

"But he answered, "It is written, "Man shall not live by bread alone, but by every word that comes from the mouth of God." - Matthew 4:4

_____
_____
_____
_____

COMPASS COMMITMENT: This is what I will personally do to commit to embracing the new ideas in this chapter will strengthen my soul toward **Scripture** activities that reflect that **Christ is my Core.**

1.

2.

3.

DIRECTING THE ARROW

This week I will place my Bible in a visible area of my home. I will commit to reading a story, chapter or verse as soon as I wake in the morning. I will also consider downloading a Bible smartphone app (see index of recommendations) or sign up for a daily scripture email reflection.

I will read and reflect on the daily Mass readings. I will journal about the thoughts that come to my heart. I will pay attention to how this new habit changes my perspectives and brings peace to the week's decisions and opportunities.

JOURNAL REFLECTIONS FROM THE WEEK:

_____
_____
_____
_____
_____
_____
_____
_____
_____
_____
_____
_____
_____
_____
_____
_____
_____
_____
_____
_____
_____

CHAPTER 7:

SACRAMENTS AND SAINTS: SOUL FOOD AND GUIDES FOR THE JOURNEY

HEBREWS: 4:16

"Let us therefore come boldly to the throne of grace, that we may obtain mercy and find grace to help in time of need."

Commercials have always been a powerful vehicle for companies who want to promote their products. Sometimes, we'll see the same commercial repeated several times a day and eventually, we equate the visuals with the messaging without even seeing the commercial. Some jingles are forever playing in our heads.

I've often wondered how different our world might be if our churches did commercials? Would the sales pitches be for greater participation in the sacraments and greater reliance on the intercession of the saints? I believe that our saints, their inspiring lives, and virtuous messages would have an even greater impact on us than probably some of our most famous actors and actresses.

We are such a visual society. The more we see and hear through popular media, the greater our emotional attachment and adoption of those messages. What we see and hear repeatedly becomes branded into our brains and eventually played out in our life choices.

Our children are spending an inordinate amount of time on their smartphones and accessing digital media throughout the day for hours at a time. Messages here are not always peace-giving. We are also engaging in these same activities more often than we probably should. If only we might consider taking some of that media time and instead, redirect it to more spiritual activities like the sacraments.

It's so important that we recognize the extraordinary power we have to redirect what is being programmed in the minds and souls of our families today, especially as they are being formed as children and into adulthood. The best way to do this is to *first* analyze our attitudes and behaviors relative to active participation in the sacraments. There is a channel of grace offering peace that we may not be accessing regularly.

Some of the catechism rules I memorized in my sacramental prep classes as a child feel sound like some of the popular commercial jingles I hear on TV. As students, we would recite the rules over and over again, sometimes even singing these definitions.

The most memorable is: *What is a Sacrament?* I can still, to this day, recite it from memory, "A sacrament is an outward sign instituted by Christ to give grace." *What is Grace?* is another spiritual jingle I recall as well. By definition, grace is, "a supernatural gift of God bestowed on us, through the merits of Jesus Christ, for our salvation." [12]

Grace remains that invisible superpower I know I need, and I just have to trust that the source of this grace is something I must seek. As a child, I had no idea that it was something I had to access. I just assumed it was inside me as a gift through Baptism. It seems possible we'd have more guidance and grace to manage any number of life situations if our souls were focused more on receiving the benefits of the sacraments.

As adults, we have numerous responsibilities on any given day to manage multiple priorities. Sacraments don't always make the list. Unfortunately, we are making our lives significantly harder because we are not taking full advantage of the grace that the sacraments were created to provide. We sometimes neglect to give prominence and priority to the sacraments that can help us the most.

As a child, Baptism, First Holy Communion, Penance, and the Sacrament of Confirmation were highly valued in my faith formation. These were really big spiritual events that were celebrated but never intended to be a one-time event. When I taught sacramental prep classes, I was so surprised to learn that many of my students had not received some of these sacraments since first receiving them.

Today, these sacraments provide powerful grace that empowers and moves us in the right direction toward God's will for our lives. Many of us are so busy trying to manage our lives by relying more on our instincts that we forget that this grace is free and available without limitations.

Grace is a peace-giving power that provides the courage and confidence to make good choices and tackle formidable obstacles in life. Parents who participate frequently in the sacraments bring more peace into their family lives.

One sacrament that is the least used, most valuable, and has the greatest return on the investment of time is the sacrament of Penance or Reconciliation. The purpose behind this practice is greatly misunderstood. Historically for Catholics, this sacrament was encouraged as a time to report our sins; sharing with a priest what we had done wrong and asking for forgiveness to start over.

There was embarrassment and shame attached to the process which is why so many have strayed from this grace-filled practice. If you've ever had an unpleasant experience; it's time to reconsider the grace you are missing and do the research to find an alternative confessor.

Jesus shared these encouraging words with Saint Faustina in her diary, *Divine Mercy in My Soul*:

"My daughter, just as you prepare in My presence, so also you make your confession before Me. The person of the priest is, for Me, only a screen. Never analyze what sort of priest it is that I am making use of; open your soul in confession as you would to Me, and I will fill it with My light." [13]

Today, priests are more interested in what is troubling you and what guidance you seek. The priest is there to help each soul to be healed and restored to a more peaceful state without sin. Great priests who can be wonderful spiritual advisors are out there waiting to support your spiritual formation.

Many adults today do not receive this sacrament often and rarely take full advantage of the opportunities for grace. The greatest benefit of cleansing our minds and hearts from those temptations that keep us from enjoying intimacy with our Father is to get *unstuck* in hurtful behaviors that we repeat often.

This sacrament was given by Jesus to His first priests, the apostles to offer merciful love, forgiveness, and the grace needed to simply live the most peaceful lives. By acknowledging our sins and wounds of the heart, we are provided with an opportunity to forgive ourselves and heal. The negative energy attached to sin is removed from the soul allowing you to be free to live in peace.

Every priest has a different style. It's important to seek out a priest who can be a trusting confidant who appeals to you if you feel awkward revisiting this opportunity. The Sacrament of Reconciliation pours new life and energy into a body and soul that is weak from sinful experiences.

This sacrament invites us to reflect on those times when we allowed negative thoughts and actions to stand in the way of loving our heavenly Father. It's a sacred time to make a sincere promise to make better choices. Loving ourselves allows us to be more at peace in our souls and love others more profoundly. This sacrament builds up the kingdom of heaven here on Earth.

If you or someone you know has ever lost weight, there's great excitement to buy new clothes that fit rather than altering the old ones. The same idea is reflected here with a confession. Shedding the old sins and habits and beginning anew with the power of God's healing is freely given to the soul in this sacrament. It is a peaceful exercise worth doing frequently.

The internet has many great examples of how to best examine your conscience with many questions provided as a guide. There are even smartphone apps today that make it even easier to keep a daily check on those times you fell from God's grace.

God longs to be in a relationship with us.

If we can remember that we are in *His* presence while the priest is simply acting as an advocate, we can approach the sacrament with more positivity and participation.

We are reminded that God loves us and forgives us without hesitation. This sacrament should become a priority to all those that want to live with a *Compass Club* mentality moving forward. Our souls are most powerfully strengthened when we receive graces from this sacred encounter.

You will be inspired to seek confession often when you make this sacrament an integral part of your faith commitment. The peace that comes to your soul will be profound.

This same passion for the sacrament of the Eucharist will also offer you a radical conversion of heart and soul. I began the habit of going to daily Mass many years ago. That daily investment of thirty minutes a day pours an abundance of peace into my soul. I can no longer go without that spiritual investment each day.

Over the past few years, attendance at Mass has declined rather dramatically. Some statistics show that less than twenty percent of registered Catholic families go to church services. The great pain and suffering the Church has experienced as a result of sinful priests who abused children and the neglect of their superiors who did not impose appropriate and timely remediation has cost the Catholic Church many followers. Great suffering has come to those families and souls that are not being spiritually nourished by the Eucharist.

When you consciously choose to participate often in a sacramental experience like the Eucharist and Reconciliation, the grace pours into your soul and there's an energy that supplies precisely what wisdom is needed in any moment of discernment. There's a peace that exudes from the soul that further drives loving actions with great confidence and clarity.

I often speak to my children about the way I feel after coming from Mass or Penance and I share the lessons I received from the homily. It's important we share those experiences with those we love and who are entrusted to our care. Even if they are not participating or believe what you are doing is for them; your witness might be the spark that lights the fire of their faith again.

Today, our society has a growing dependence on drugs and alcohol for easing anxiety and stress. The statistics are alarming and reflect a growing reliance on using these substances. We shockingly remain depressed, overwhelmed, and unhappy even though as a society, many enjoy a plentitude of rich resources.

It seems plausible that inner peace might be more attainable with a *greater reliance* on spiritual tools, resources, and sacramental experiences like Penance, the Mass, and the Eucharist that can empower the mind and enrich the soul with a more peaceful disposition. It's certainly worth consideration and there are no negative side effects.

There are thousands of books, websites, and podcasts today that focus on the power of meditation. The sacraments, however, also provide a strong foundation for meditative prayer as a solution for tranquility. When I started going to mass beyond my Sunday obligation, I felt a strong gravitational pull there.

There are certainly people in our world who have psychological and medical needs that require the right medication, but there are also many who have been blessed by the spiritual healing benefits received from the sacraments. The Liturgy of the Word and the Liturgy of the Eucharist have given much comfort and offered new soulful insights to those suffering from self-doubt, shame, and hopelessness.

The gravitational pull of the world and the accompanying pressures are no longer so daunting for a soul that is nourished often with an infusion of sacramental grace. If you ask anyone who goes to daily Mass, Reconciliation, and receives the Eucharist regularly why they do so, they'll typically say that they *go for the grace*. That grace keeps them grounded and peaceful in mind, body, and spirit.

It's a treasure we need to take seriously if we want what God wants. There's a reason these three sacraments are called the *living sacraments*. Their impact breathes life into the soul.

As a society, we also spend millions of dollars each year on improving our physical appearances. We find ways to enhance our well-being with dietary supplements as well as beauty and fitness regimens. The commercials and the jingles make it hard to ignore the latest and greatest feel-good cure.

Grace is something we can't see but if we believe the power of grace can enhance our lives and direct our energy more positively, we will learn that other enhancements fair in comparison. In Hebrews 4:16 we are reminded and encouraged to "*boldly* come to the throne of grace." *That throne is housed in the sacraments.*

God wants us to come *often* and with great passion and confidence. He created these sacraments to benefit our souls, but He won't force us to access the grace. Ultimately, our free will was given to us so we could have the freedom to choose our path. There are no guarantees that the path will be free of challenges, but if our soul is sanctified with grace, we will feel far less anxious about our ultimate destination.

It's worth noting here that *the way* we approach our participation in these sacraments also has a direct cause-effect relationship on the outcome. If we go to Mass with expectations to be entertained by a compelling sermon, we might be disappointed and never go back. Many of my former students shared that Mass was boring which is why they and their parents did not always attend services.

Recognizing that this is a holy and sacred sacramental experience should motivate us to approach the experience differently than we'd encounter a secular or social event. If we simply go to Mass because we are obligated, we will never be truly satisfied. When we go to Mass and actually feel the presence of our holy and loving God and fully embrace the symbolism this celebration represents, our souls can truly reap the benefits.

When we give God permission to sit alongside us and speak to our soul, we will be transformed. We won't care if the sermon was long or short. We won't even notice if the music was to our preferences. There will be no judgment, only intimacy with the Lord in such a way that we will crave it the next time. This is how this sacrament becomes a spiritual gift of grace and peace.

If heaven truly is our goal, grace has got to be the *one non-negotiable* tool in our toolbox. It seems logical that more frequent participation in these sacraments might be a good idea, especially if we do not feel at peace in our lives. For those that choose the *Compass Club* way of life, *it's the lifeline*.

When the grace of God is inside us, there's no other spirit that can distract us from the truth of God's Word. In 1 Corinthians 3:16-17 we are reminded that we are "temples of the Holy Spirit." Well, God can't dwell in us if we lack the grace to keep Him there. Strengthen your soul toward peace with the power of the sacraments.

The saints, above all, embraced the fruits of the Holy Spirit and the accompanying graces by participating in the sacraments *fully* and *often.* Anyone who has ever read about the lives of the saints couldn't possibly imagine living as courageously and as selflessly as they did or even having the impact on the world as they did.

I think many of us might say, "I could never be a saint. I could never be that holy." Saints also *suffered* greatly for their witness. Who wants to suffer? Certainly, no one I know would ever deliberately desire to suffer for the honor of being called a saint.

They did, however, embrace very challenging life experiences and they enjoyed *unfathomable peace.* Today, we can learn so much from their lives. Inviting them to guide us on our earthly journey by *praying to them* and asking for their divine intercession is always a great decision.

These saints were just ordinary people like us who did extraordinary things. The joy they still experienced despite many crosses came from the blessing of the gifts of the Holy Spirit. *It was their focus on Christ that was their common denominator.*

In Galatians 5:22-23, we are reminded, "The fruits of the Spirit are love, joy, peace, patience, kindness, generosity, faithfulness, gentleness, and self-control." By modeling ourselves like the saints that have gone before us, we will be inspired to live in a way that allows us to share these gifts with our world as they did.

They lived like Christ and loved as He did. They experienced an abundance of inner peace. They consistently remained humble in their abilities and instead relied entirely on the power of grace to move their intentions forward. That seems like a reasonable goal. We should consider their life examples.

They never planned to be holy, but they were given that distinction by their steadfast obedience and abiding love of their Divine Creator. *They kept Christ as their core and strengthened their souls with the grace of God every day of their lives.*

They were far from perfect; they sinned, made mistakes, and sometimes, even felt abandoned, but they remained focused and they persevered. They placed the highest value on frequent participation in the Mass and the sacraments of Penance and the Eucharist.

They were, however, holy and ordinary, so it makes sense we *might* want to direct our prayerful intentions to live in their ways, but also *boldly* ask for their intercession in our lives.

Many of them are recognized for their intercession for special intentions. Some are more popular than others. There is a saint we can pray to every day of the year.

Some of the most popular include Saint Mother Teresa (*doubters*), Saint Jude (*hopeless causes*), Saint Padre Pio (*suffering*), Saint Peregrine (*cancer*), Saint Michael/Saint Benedict (*protection*), Saint Christopher (*travel*), Saint Rita (*marriage*), Saint Francis (*the poor*), Saint Gianna (*sanctity of life*), Saint Joseph (*family*), Saint Gertrude (*souls in purgatory*) and Saint Therese, the Little Flower (*simplicity*) are some of the most well-known and popular saints of our time.

Today, there are helpful smartphone applications that give us frequent access to the lives of the saints and their prayers that facilitate intentional focus and requests for their intercession. Remembering to focus our arrows on the intention of keeping these saints alive in our daily lives by praying to them and learning more about them yields powerful spiritual benefits.

One specific way we can invite their intercession is by praying a *novena*. A novena is a series of prayers lasting nine days that dates back to the Ascension when our Blessed Mother and the apostles were in the upper room praying for nine days that lead up to the Pentecost (Acts 1:14). Today, this practice is a popular and effective way to call on the support and intercession of the saints.

The website, *Pray More Novenas* (see index), offers a daily email service that updates subscribers and invites participation for novenas assigned to every saint. It's an easy and consistent way to remember to pray to them.

Certainly, the saints experienced great suffering and pain is not very appealing, but their *alignment of that suffering* to the wounds of Christ brought powerful benefits to their souls and directed their actions honorably.

When we read about the lives of the saints, we always learn that somehow, they were peace-filled and joyful in the midst of their suffering. How did they do that? What was their secret?

We should want that knowledge because suffering is a reality in our chaotic world and navigating that reality is a necessity. Perhaps we might consider using them as heavenly life coaches.

The saints can make a big difference in the way we handle suffering now and hardships that might be coming in the future. Finding ways to accept suffering as a means to immeasurable graces can be a strategic decision we make daily as the saints so capably mastered.

Wikipedia reflects that, "In Christianity, the word "saint" refers to any person who is "in Christ", and in whom Christ dwells, whether in Heaven or in earth." [14]

There's so much we can learn from the lives of the saints that we can apply to our lives here on earth. We have the unique opportunity to be part of their *communion of saints* if we model their behavior, focus prayerfully, and embrace the sacraments as they did during their lifetimes.

They lived in the light of the love of Christ because they followed His commandments and took full advantage of the grace that came from frequent participation in the sacraments. Those of us who seek the prayerful intercession and protection of the saints will find the same peace they enjoyed.

Let's plan on seeking holiness and strengthening our souls with their help daily. This is the best way to ensure we are living intentionally to be our *holiest* selves as they did and in full accordance with the will of God.

The former Archbishop of Philadelphia, Charles Joseph Chaput, OFM Cap wrote an impactful pastoral letter in 2014 that truly reflected his goals for the mission of the Archdiocese of Philadelphia school system to *"equip saints for life."*

The Greek words en the os or "God within," remind us that the life of God within us, a heartfelt Catholic enthusiasm for our mission, is the best proof to our students that we care for them. Witnessing to the life of God in our own hearts inspires those around us to do the same. Thus, we do not ask our teachers to simply "enjoy" what they do but instead to live honestly and visibly as disciples of Jesus Christ.

Being aware that Baptism by itself does not make a Christian living and acting in conformity with the Gospel is necessary – the Catholic school tries to create within its walls a climate in which the pupil's faith will gradually mature and enable him to assume the responsibility placed on him by Baptism. [15]

His words of advice apply to all of us who have a moral responsibility to not just live the mission given uniquely to each one of us according to our unique gifts but even more so, *sharing that witness with those we guide and teach.*

Archbishop Chaput reiterates that the tantamount responsibility we all have is to go *beyond the grace* given to us at Baptism and *increase our reliance* on the Gospel to guide us. In this way, we are equipping ourselves to be saints and modeling for those that are entrusted to our care.

In Baptism, we are given the grace of the sacrament as well as the gifts of the Holy Spirit. These gifts of wisdom, understanding, knowledge, piety, fortitude, fear of the Lord, and counsel will not be cultivated to their fullest potential without prayer, the sacraments, and living like the saints—*our spirit guides for our journey.*

Father Bartunek talks about these gifts from God to the baptized person in his book, *A Quiet Place-How Daily Prayer Can Change your Life*:

> They are not just feelings we have or actions to perform; they are spiritual forces present and active in us through grace. These are ingredients of lasting happiness.
> These are the spiritual qualities that make life worth living, that produce healthy family life, that overflow into the forging of a strong and creative culture. They are what we feel called to live but constantly find ourselves falling short of living. [16]

In the index, there is a link to the *Discernment of Gifts in the Spirit Inventory* that is highly recommended you complete. Knowing what gifts God has given you will further enhance your life direction and bring more abundant peace to your life trajectory.

You might also have your family members complete it. Creating an environment in the home that nurtures and strengthens these gifts will give greater clarity for the life mission of each family member.

Once you embrace these gifts and begin the intentional process of developing them further, you will strongly impact your family and those entrusted to your care outside the home and the world. This is the responsibility of all of us as children of God to build up the kingdom on Earth.

The saints may not have had a questionnaire to tell them the gifts they possessed, but they had a clear *vision of their mission*. They were filled with the Spirit of God. Their spiritual gifts gave them peace no matter how much they suffered. The arrows of their souls remained directed toward the promise and hope of Heaven.

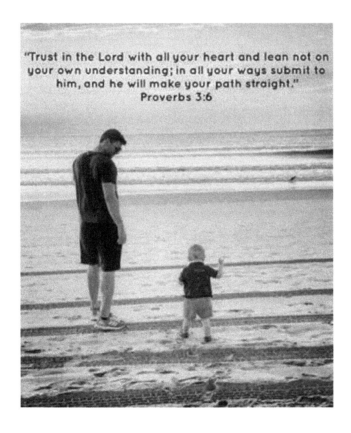

"Trust in the Lord with all your heart and lean not on your own understanding; in all your ways submit to him, and he will make your path straight."
Proverbs 3:6

COMPASS CONNECTIONS: Reflect on the following scripture passages and write down specific ways you can apply these bible messages to your **Sacraments** practice as part of your new Compass living strategy:

"Don't you know that you yourselves are God's temple and that God's Spirit dwells in your midst? If anyone destroys God's temple, God will destroy that person; for God's temple is sacred, and you together are that temple." - 1 Corinthians 6: 19-20

_____
_____
_____
_____

"The Spirit who lives in you is greater than the spirit who lives in the world." - 1 John 4:4

_____
_____
_____
_____

"Every good and perfect gift is from above and comes down from the Father of lights, with who there is no variation of shadow turning." - James 1: 17

_____
_____
_____
_____

"As the Father has loved me, so have I loved you. Abide in my love. If you keep my commandments, you will abide in my love, just as I have kept my Father's commandments and abide in his love. These things I have spoken to you, that my joy may be in you, and that your joy may be full." - John 15: 9-11

_____
_____
_____
_____

COMPASS COMMITMENT: This is what I will personally do to commit to embracing the new ideas in this chapter will strengthen my soul toward **Sacramental** activities that support that **Christ is my Core.**

1.

2.

3.

DIRECTING THE ARROW

This week I will go to Confession and receive the Sacrament of Reconciliation (Penance) to give my soul a clean slate and the opportunity to receive an abundance of grace. I will get a referral from an active parishioner if I'm feeling apprehensive.

I will also go to *one* additional Mass celebration this week in addition to my Sunday obligation. I will go back to Church if I have been absent using some of the new insights I have received.

COMPASS CONNECTIONS: Reflect on the following scripture passages and write down specific ways you can apply these bible messages to your **Saints** practice as part of your new Compass living strategy:

"Therefore I, the prisoner of the Lord, implore you to walk in a manner worthy of the calling with which you have been called, with all humility and gentleness, with patience, showing tolerance for one another in love, being diligent to preserve the unity of the Spirit in the bond of peace." - Ephesians 4:1-3

_____
_____
_____
_____

"Here is the perseverance of the saints who keep the commandments of God and their faith in Jesus." - Revelation 14:12

_____
_____
_____
_____

"As for the saints who are in the earth, they are the majestic ones in who is all my delight." - Psalm 16:3

_____
_____
_____
_____

"But the saints of the Highest One will receive the kingdom and possess the kingdom forever, for all ages to come." - Daniel 7:18

_____
_____
_____
_____
_____

COMPASS COMMITMENT: This is what I will personally do to commit to embracing the new ideas in this chapter will strengthen my soul toward **Saints** activities that support **Christ is my Core.**

1.

2.

3.

DIRECTING THE ARROW

This week I will download any smartphone resource that offers a **Saint of the Day** reflections or I will sign up for a **Saint of the Day** email subscription to become more proactive in learning more about the lives of the saints. I will commit to praying for their intercession and guidance. I will also pray to the patron saint I chose when I received the Sacrament of Confirmation and make a bigger commitment to pray to this saint daily.

JOURNAL REFLECTIONS FOR THE WEEK:

_____
_____
_____
_____
_____
_____
_____
_____
_____
_____
_____
_____
_____
_____
_____
_____
_____
_____
_____
_____
_____
_____
_____

Finally, as parents, caretakers, and educators, we are all charged with an apostolic duty to be our best selves. We feel true joy when we bring out the best qualities in those we love and are charged to care for. We intrinsically know when we are off-balance. We have peace in our minds and exude joy and love when we are making good choices.

People who see us living in balance like this become curious. *They want what we have*. This is how we live our faith and share it.

In John 20:19 we remember that the most profound and simple greeting Jesus offered to His apostles after His resurrection was; "Peace be with you." *This same peace He desires for us today*. He desires to share His love and bring light to our path as He walks alongside us.

As members of the *Compass Club*, let us welcome the most saints into heaven that we possibly can so that when it's our time to return to heaven, we will also hear the words spoken by God to His Son, "And a voice from heaven said, This, is My beloved Son, in who I am well pleased" (Matt. 3:17).

God will also be pleased with us if we have kept His beloved Son as the core of our compass and our souls remained strong in our daily witness. St. Paul encourages this in Philippians 1: 3-6, "I am confident of this, that the one who began a good work in you will continue to complete it until the day of Christ Jesus."

All of the angels and saints will rejoice in welcoming us back to our eternal home because we followed a path that *completed the good work placed in us*, we remain devoted to our Blessed Mother and her Son, enlisted the guidance of the Holy Spirit and the saints and lastly, we received abundant grace from the sacraments often.

The formula for a more peaceful life is pretty simple. We just need to consistently say, "yes" to God's calling and trust that no matter what challenges or suffering comes our way, it's part of a much bigger plan that will be revealed to us someday. We need patience and trust to embrace the journey. *That's what faith is.*

Father Jacques Philippe provides a beautiful meditation on peace in his book, *In the School of the Spirit*:

> The Spirit of God is a spirit of peace, and He speaks and acts in peace and gentleness, never in tumult and agitation. What's more, the motions of the Spirit are delicate touches that don't make a great noise and can penetrate our spiritual consciousness only if we have within ourselves a sort of calm zone of silence and peace. If our inner world is noisy and agitated, the gentle voice of the Holy Spirit will find it very difficult to be heard. If we want to recognize and follow the Spirit's motions, it is of the greatest importance to maintain a peaceful heart in all circumstances. [17]

I hope the *calm zone of silence and peace* that Father Philippe speaks of will be yours everyday of your life. I pray that you will hear that gentle voice of the Holy Spirit guiding your steps along your path that stays illuminated today and all the days of your life with the love of Christ as the core of your being. *Keep your soul strong.* Take this message to those you love. Above all, may the peace of Christ be with you always.

I give thanks to my God at every remembrance of you,

praying always with joy in my every prayer for all of you,

because of your partnership for the Gospel

from the first day until now.

I am confident of this,

that the one who began a good work in you

will continue to complete it

until the day of Christ Jesus.

It is right that I should think this way about all of you,

because I hold you in my heart,

you who are all partners with me in grace,

both in my imprisonment

and in the defense and confirmation of the Gospel.

For God is my witness,

how I long for all of you with the affection of Christ Jesus.

And this is my prayer:

that your love may increase ever more and more

in knowledge and every kind of perception,

to discern what is of value,

so that you may be pure and blameless for the day of Christ,

filled with the fruit of righteousness

that comes through Jesus Christ

for the glory and praise of God.

-St. Paul's Letter to the Philippians
Philippians 1: 3-11

NOTES

1. Tim Gray, Praying Scripture for a Change (Pennsylvania: Ascension Press, 2009), 36

2. Catechism of the Catholic Church (New York: First Image Books by Doubleday, 1997), 665

3. Congregation of the Sisters of Our Lady of Mercy, Divine Mercy in My Soul, Diary of Saint Maria Faustina Kowalska (Massachusetts: Marian Press, 2011), 81

4. Louis de Montfort, Secret of the Rosary (New York: Montfort Publications, 1992), 7

5. America Needs Fatima, The Rosary (Pennsylvania: The American Society for the Defense of Tradition, Family and Property, 2020), 82

6. Congregation of the Sisters of Our Lady of Mercy, Divine Mercy in My Soul, Diary of Saint Maria Faustina Kowalska (Massachusetts: Marian Press, 2011), 609-610

7. The Padre Pio Foundation of America, My Saint Pio Prayer Book (Connecticut, 1977), 44

8. Father Slavko Barbaric, O.F.M. Fasting (Medjugorje: Medjugorje Web, 2020), 32

9. The Sisters of the Visitation and Saint Margaret Mary Alacoquo, Autobiography of Saint Margaret Mary, (North Carolina: Tan Books, 1995), 9

10. Catechism of the Catholic Church (New York: First Image Books by Doubleday, 1997), 693

11. Susan Conroy, Praying with Mother Teresa (Massachusetts: Marian Press, 2016), 136

12. Catechism of the Catholic Church (New York: First Image Books by Doubleday, 1997), 539

13. Congregation of the Sisters of Our Lady of Mercy, Divine Mercy in My Soul, Diary of Saint Maria Faustina Kowalska (Massachusetts: Marian Press, 2011), 568-569

14. Wikipedia Foundation, Definition of Christianity (Wikipedia.org, 2021)

15. Archbishop Charles Joseph Chaput, OFM, Equipping Saints for Life Pastoral Letter (Pennsylvania: Catholic Philly.com, 2014)

16. Fr. John Bartunek, A Quiet Place How Daily Prayer Can Change Your Life (Florida: Beacon Publishing, 2017), 6-7

17. Father Jacques Philippe, In the School of the Spirit (New York: Scepter Publishers, 2017), 137

DIRECTING THE ARROW OF THE SOUL
Supplemental Scripture Passages

1. My flesh and my heart may fail, but God is the strength of my heart and my portion forever. Psalm 73:26

2. Whoever says he abides in Him ought to walk in the same way in which He walked. 1 John 2:6

3. And after you have suffered a little while, The God of all grace, who has called you to his eternal glory in Christ, will himself restore, confirm, strengthen, and establish you. 1 Peter 5:10

4. For to this you have been called, because Christ also suffered for you, leaving you an example, so that you might follow in His steps. 1 Peter 2:21

5. So as to walk in a manner worth of the Lord, fully pleasing to Him, bearing fruit in every good work and increasing in the knowledge of God. Colossians 1:10

6. I have said these things to you, that in me you may have peace. In the world you will have tribulation. But take heart; I have overcome the world. John 16:33

7. Fear not, for I am with you; be not dismayed, for I am your God; I will strengthen you, I will help you, I will uphold you with my righteous right hand. Isaiah 41:10

8. Have I not commanded you? Be strong and courageous. Do not be frightened, and do not be dismayed, for the Lord your God is with you wherever you go. Joshua 1:9

9. I can do all things through him who strengthens me. Philippians 4:13

10. But they who wait for the Lord shall renew their strength; they shall mount up with wings like eagles; they shall run and not be weary; they shall walk and not faint. Isaiah 40:31

11. Be strong and courageous. Do not fear or be in dread of them, for it is the Lord your God who goes with you. He will not leave you or forsake you. Deuteronomy 31:6

12. That according to the riches of his glory he may grant you to be strengthened with power through his Spirit in your inner being. Ephesians 3:16

13. Seek the Lord and his strength; seek his presence continually! 1 Corinthians 16:11

14. For the sake of Christ, then, I am content with weaknesses, insults, hardships, persecutions, and calamities. For when I am weak, then I am strong. 2 Corinthians 12:20

15. Count it all joy, my brothers, when you meet trials of various kinds, for you know that the testing of your faith produces steadfastness. James 1: 2-3

16. On the day I called, you answered me; my strength of soul you increased. Psalm 128:3

17. Only let your manner of life be worthy of the gospel of Christ, so that whether I come and see you or am absent, I may hear of you that you are standing firm in one spirit, with one mind striving by side for the faith of the gospel. Philippians 1:27

COMPASS CLUB APPENDIX AND RESOURCES FOR EVERYDAY REFERENCE:

Daily Readings, Prayers and Media Resources:

Discernment of the Gifts of the Holy Spirit: Diocese of Cleveland
https://diolc.org/wp-content/uploads/2017/05/Spiritual-Gifts-Inventory-Assessment-Diocese-of-Cleveland-ICSC.pdf

How to Pray Lectio Divina
https://bustedhalo.com/ministry-resources/lectio-divina-beginners-guide

National Catholic Register
https://www.catholicnewsagency.com

The Living Word
https://subscriptions.liguori.org/Shop/ViewCatOC.aspx?sel=5

The Magnificat
https://us.magnificat.net/home

The Word Among Us
https://www.wau.org

United Council of Catholic Bishops:
https://www.uscb.org

Pray More Novenas
https://www.praymorenovenas.com/

The Surrender Novena
https://healingheartofjesus.com/2019/01/03/the-surrender-novena/

COMPASS CLUB PRAYERS AND DAILY SCHEDULE SUGGESTIONS:

Morning:
- Morning Offering
- Fiat of the Eternal Father
- Chosen Prayer
- The Jesus Prayer

Daily Mass:
- Body and Blood of Christ Booklet: www.columban.org

Mid-Day:
- Angelus:
  https://www.ewtn.com/catholicism/devotions/angelus-383

Divine Mercy Hour: 3pm-4pm:
- Divine Mercy Chaplet: https://www.thedivinemercy.org
- The Holy Rosary: https://therosary.online/prayers/

Evening:
- Examination of Conscience:
  https://fathersofmercy.com/wp-content/uploads/2020/03/2020Examination.pdf

Morning Offering:
Written in 1844 by Fr. Fracois-Savier Gautrelet
https://www.ewtn.com/catholicism/devotions/morning-offering-394

Oh Jesus, through the Immaculate Heart of Mary, I offer you my prayers, joys, and sufferings of this day for all the intentions of your Sacred Heart, in union with the Holy Sacrifice of the Mass throughout the world, for the salvation of souls, the reparation of sins, the reunion of all Christians and in particular for the intentions of the Holy Father. Amen.

Fiat of the Eternal Father

https://www.maryscall.com/prayer-cards

My Beloved Father
Thy will be done on earth as it is in Heaven.
Be Thou my Father. Be always my Eternal Father.
Do not leave my soul. Do not abandon me. Do not leave me out
of your sight, my Father, for I am Your child, whom You have
created to please You, to adore You, to honor You, living my
days as You have given e license to live it.
(I offer this Fiat through Mary, to Jesus, to You, Eternal Father.)

Chosen Prayer

https://www.joemelendrez.com

Jesus, I accept your invitation to heaven. You chose to save me
not because of what I've done, but because of who you are. I
freely give my life to you. I pray to know you deeper and trust in
your plan. I will continue to show up, even when it's tough. I am
your instrument. If you can use anyone, you can use me. I place
my faith in you. I will share the love you've given to me so that
others may know you. I will be a light for the world. I am a
chosen child of God. Amen

The Jesus Prayer

https://www.ourcatholicprayers.com/jesus-prayer.html

Jesus Christ, Son of the living God, have mercy on me a sinner.

Hail Mary

https://www.ewtn.com/catholicism/devotions/hail-mary-348

Hail Mary, full of grace. The Lord is with you. Blessed are you
among women and blessed is the fruit of thy womb, Jesus. Holy
Mary, Mother of God pray for us sinners, now and at the hour of
our death. Amen.

Serenity Prayer
Written by American theologian, Reinhold Niebuhr

https://www.archspm.org/faith-and-discipleship/prayer/catholic-prayers/the-serenity-prayer/

God, grant me the serenity to accept the things I cannot change, courage to change the things I can, and the wisdom to know the difference. Living one day at a time; enjoying one moment at a time; accepting hardships as the pathway to peace; Taking as Jesus did, this sinful world as it is, not as I would have it. Trusting that He will make all things right if I surrender to His Will. That I may be reasonably happy in this life and supremely happy with Him forever in the next. Amen.

Peace Prayer of Saint Francis

https://www.loyolapress.com/catholic-resources/prayer/traditional-catholic-prayers/saints-prayers/peace-prayer-of-saint-francis/

Lord, make me an instrument of your peace: where there is hatred, let me sow love; where there is injury, pardon; where there is doubt, faith; where there is despair, hope; where there is darkness, light; where there is sadness, joy. Oh, divine master, grant that I may not so much seek to be consoled as to console, to be understood as to understand, to be loved as to love. For it is in giving that we receive, it is in pardoning that we are pardoned, and it is in dying that we are born to eternal life. Amen

The Spiritual Communion Prayer
Written by St. Alphonsus Liguori

https://www.vaticannews.v/en/prayers/the-spiritual-communion.html

My Jesus, I believe that You are present in the Most Blessed Sacrament. I love You above all things, and I desire to receive You into my soul. Since I cannot now receive you sacramentally, come at least spiritually into my heart. I embrace You as if you were already there, and I unite myself wholly to You. Never permit me to be separately from You.

The Golden Arrow Prayer
(revealed by Our Lord to Carmelite Nun St. Mary of St. Peter of Tours 1843)
https://www.theworkofgod.org/Prayers/Treasure.asp?page=84

May the most holy, most sacred, most adorable, most incomprehensible and ineffable Name of God be forever praised, blessed, loved, adored and glorified in Heaven, on Earth, and under the Earth by all the creatures of God and by the Sacred Heart of Our Lord Jesus Christ in the Most Holy Sacrament of the Altar. Amen.

15 Second Gratitude Prayer
Written by Father Rob Galea
https://www.frgministry.com/home

Lord, I just want to thank you for the goodness of your presence in my life even though I cannot see you, even though I cannot hear you. I know you are present. Bless me, bless my family. Guide me and give me a heart that is grateful. I ask this Blessing in the Name of the Father and the Son and the Holy Spirit. Amen

Holy Spirit Prayer
https://www.acatholic.org/traditional-catholic-prayers/catholic-prayers-to-the-holy-spirit/

Come Holy Spirit, fill the hearts of Your faithful, and kindle in them the fire of your love. Send forth Your Spirit and they shall be created, and You shall renew the face of the earth.
Oh God, who by the light of the Holy Spirit, did instruct the hearts of your faithful, grant that by the gift of the Holy Spirit, we may be truly wise and always rejoice in His consolation through Christ our Lord, Amen.

Guardian Angel Prayer
https://www.ewtn.com/catholicism/devotions/prayer-to-your-guardian-angel-373

Angel of God my Guardian dear, to whom God's love entrust me here. Ever this day be at my side, to light, to guide, to rule. Amen

St. Michael, the Archangel

https://www.ewtn.com/catholicism/devotions/prayer-to-st-michael-the-archangel-371

St. Michael the Archangel defend us in battle. Be our protection against the wickedness and snares of the devil. May God rebuke him. We humbly pray. Do thou oh Prince of the Heavenly Hosts by the power of God, cast into hell Satan and all his evil followers that prowl around the world seeking the ruin of souls. Amen.

Memorare Prayer

https://www.ourcatholicprayers.com/memorare.html

Remember, O most gracious Virgin Mary, that never was it known that anyone who fled to your protection, implored your help, or sought your intercession was left unaided. Inspired by this confidence I fly unto you, O virgin of virgins, my Mother. To you do I come, before you I stand, sinful and sorrowful. O Mother of the Word Incarnate, despise not my petitions, but in your mercy, hear and answer me. Amen

Hail Holy Queen

https://www.loyolapress.com/catholic-resources/prayer/traditional-catholic-prayers/prayers-honoring-mary/hail-holy-queen-prayer/

Hail, holy Queen, Mother of mercy,
hail, our life, our sweetness, and our hope.
To you we cry, the children of Eve;
to you we send up our sighs,
mourning and weeping in this land of exile.
Turn, then, most gracious advocate,
your eyes of mercy toward us;
lead us home at last
and show us the blessed fruit of your womb, Jesus:
O clement, O loving, O sweet Virgin Mary.

The Angelus (*pray at 12 noon daily*)

https://www.ourcatholicprayers.com/the-angelus.html

V. The Angel of the Lord declared unto Mary;
R. And she conceived by the Holy Spirit.
Recite Hail Mary Prayer

V. Behold the handmaid of the Lord.
R. Be it done unto me according to your word.
Recite Hail Mary Prayer

V. And the Word was made flesh.
R. And dwelt among us.
Recite Hail Mary Prayer

V. Pray for us Holy Mother of God,
R. That we made be made worthy of the promises of Christ.

V. Let us pray
R. Pour forth, we beseech you, O Lord, your grace into our hearts, that we, to whom the incarnation of Christ, your Son, was made known by the message of an angel, may by his passion and cross be brought to the glory of his resurrection, through the same Christ our Lord. Amen.

The Unity Prayer

www.flameoflove.us

My Adorable, Jesus, may our feet journey together. May our hands gather in unity. May our hearts beat in unison. May our souls be in harmony. May our thoughts be as one. May our ears listen to the silence together. May our glances profoundly penetrate each other. May our lips pray together to gain mercy from the Eternal Father. Oh, Blessed Lady, Spread the effect of grace of thy Flame of Love over all of humanity.

Prayer of Saint Gertrude (releases 1,000 souls from Purgatory)

https://www.goodcatholic.com/prayer-for-the-holy-souls-in-purgatory-by-st-gertrude-the-great/

Eternal Father; I offer you the Most Precious Blood of Thy Divine Son, in union with the Masses said throughout the world today, for all the Holy Souls in Purgatory, for sinners everywhere, for sinners in the Universal Church, my own home and my family. Amen.

Act of Contrition

(prayed during Confession and before receiving the Eucharist)
https://www.catholic.org/prayers/prayer.php?p=43

O my God,
I am heartily sorry for having offended Thee, and I detest all my sins, because I dread the loss of heaven, and the pains of hell; but most of all because they offend Thee, my God, who are all good and deserving of my love. I firmly resolve, with the help of Thy grace, to confess my sins, to do penance, and to amend my life. Amen

My God, I am sorry for my sins with all my heart. In choosing to do wrong and failing to do good, I have sinned against You whom I should love above all things. I firmly intend with your help to do penance, to sin no more, and to avoid whatever leads to sin. Jesus Christ suffered and died for us. In His name, my God, have mercy.

The Apostles' Creed

https://www.catholic.org/prayers/prayer.php?p=220

I believe in God, the Father Almighty, Creator of heaven and earth, and in Jesus Christ, His only Son, our Lord Who was conceived by the Holy Spirit, born of the Virgin Mary, suffered under Pontius Pilate, was crucified, died and was buried; H

He descended into Hell; on the third day He rose again from the dead; He ascended into heaven and is seated at the right hand of God the Father almighty; from there He will come to judge the living and the dead.

I believe in the Holy Spirit, the holy Catholic Church, the communion of Saints, the forgiveness of sins, the resurrection of the body, and life everlasting. Amen.

Novena to the Sacred Heart of Jesus

Composed by St. Margaret Mary Alacoque and was the favorite prayer of daily petition by Saint Padre Pio

https://www.padrepio.org/pray/efficacious-novena/

O my Jesus, you have said, "Truly I say to you, ask and you will receive, seek and you will find, knock and it will be opened to you." Behold I knock, I seek and ask for the grace of … (*insert your intention here.)*

Our Father…Hail Mary…Glory be to the Father…Sacred Heart of Jesus, I place all my trust in you.

O my Jesus, you have said, "Truly I say to you, if you ask anything of the Father in my name, He will give it to you." Behold, in your name, I ask the Father for the grace of (insert your intention here.)

Our Father…Hail Mary…Glory be to the Father…Sacred Heart of Jesus, I place all my trust in you.

O my Jesus, you have said, "Truly I say to you, heaven and earth will pass away but my words will not pass away." Encouraged by your infallible words I now ask for the grace of (insert your intention here.)

Our Father…Hail Mary…Glory be to the Father…Sacred Heart of Jesus, I place all my trust in you.

O Sacred Heart of Jesus, for whom it is impossible not to have compassion on the afflicted, have pity on us miserable sinners and grant us the grace which we ask of you, through the Sorrowful and Immaculate Heart of Mary, your tender mother and ours.

Say the Hail, Holy Queen and add: St. Joseph, foster father of Jesus, pray for us.

How to Pray the Rosary

https://www.osv.com/wp-content/uploads/2021/02/howtorosary.pdf

Make the Sign of the Cross
In the name of the Father, and of the Son, and the Holy Spirit.
Amen

The Apostles' Creed
I believe in God, the Father Almighty, Creator of heaven and earth, and in Jesus Christ, His only Son, our Lord Who was conceived by the Holy Spirit, born of the Virgin Mary, suffered under Pontius Pilate, was crucified, died and was buried; He descended into Hell; on the third day He rose again from the dead; He ascended into heaven and is seated at the right hand of God the Father almighty; from there He will come to judge the living and the dead. I believe in the Holy Spirit, the holy Catholic Church, the communion of Saints, the forgiveness of sins, the resurrection of the body, and life everlasting. Amen.

The Lord's Prayer
Our Father, who art in heaven, hallowed be thy name; thy kingdom come; thy will be done on earth as it is in heaven. Give us this day our daily bread; and forgive us our trespasses as we forgive those who trespass against us; and lead us not into temptation but deliver us from evil.

Hail Mary
Hail Mary, full of grace. The Lord is with thee. Blessed art thou among women, and blessed is the fruit of thy womb, Jesus. Holy Mary, Mother of God, pray for us sinners, now and at the hour of death. Amen.

The Glory Be (The Doxology)
Glory be to the Father, and to the Son, and to the Holy Spirit. As it was in the beginning, is now, and ever shall be, world without end. Amen.

Fatima Invocation

Oh, my Jesus, forgive us our sins, save us from the fires of hell, and lead all souls to heaven, especially those most in need of thy mercy

Chaplet of Divine Mercy

(recited on ordinary Rosary beads with five decades)

https://www.thedivinemercy.org/message/devotions/pray-the-chaplet

Make the Sign of the Cross

In the name of the Father, and of the Son, and the Holy Spirit.
Amen

Optional Opening Prayers

You expired, Jesus, but the source of life gushed forth for souls,
and the ocean of mercy opened up for the whole world. O Fount
of Life, unfathomable Divine Mercy, envelope the whole world
and empty yourself upon us.

O Blood and Water, which gushed forth from the Heart of Jesus
as a fount of Mercy, I trust in You! (repeat 3 times)

Our Father, Hail Mary, and the Apostle's Creed
For each of the 5 decades: (on each of the 10 Hail Mary beads,
pray)

*For the Sake of His sorrowful Passion, have mercy on us and the whole
world.*

Concluding Prayer:
Holy God, Holy Mighty One, Holy Immortal One, have mercy
on us and the whole world. (recite 3 times)

Optional Closing Prayer

Eternal God, in who mercy is endless and the treasury of
compassion inexhaustible, look kindly upon us and increase your
mercy in us, that in difficult moments we might not despair nor
become despondent, but with great confidence submit ourselves
to Your holy will, which is Love and Mercy itself.

Prayer on a Fasting Day

Adapted and borrowed from Father Slavko Barbaric

https://enteringintothemystery.blogspot.com/2019/03/father-slavkos-prayer-for-fasting.html

Father, today I resolve to fast. In doing so, I do not despise your creation, I do not renounce it-I only want to discover their value. I choose to fast because your prophets fasted, because your Son, Jesus Christ fasted, as did His apostles and disciples. Help me to become a better disciple of your Son. I decide to fast because your servant, Mother Mary also faster. I fast today as a disciple of your Son and I ask for the intercession of the saints and my guardian angel.

Father, I present this day of fasting to you for the ability to discover your Word more and discover what is essential and non-essential in this life. I present this fast to you for Peace. -for peace in my heart, peace with my family, peace with my neighbors, peace in my town/city, state and my country. I fast for peace in the world, for all the troubled spots in the world.

I present this fast to you for reparation; reparation for my past and reparation for our society. I pray that those who do not know your Son, Jesus Christ, may be brought into contact with Him, through one of your disciples. I pray that I may be an instrument of your peace. I remember those who are hungry and impoverished.

Through this fast cleanse me of all bad habits and calm down my passions and let your virtues increase in me. Let the depth of my soul open to your grace through this fast, so that it may totally affect and cleanse me. Help me realize that fasting is not a competition and other people should not experience penance or any grumpiness from me because of my fasting. Fasting should not take away from my daily work and grant me the wisdom to know my limits. Father, please help me fast with my heart.

Mary, you were free in your heart and bound to nothing except the Father's will. Please obtain by prayer the grace of a joyful fast for me today. Let every evil and any temptation be kept away from me today through your intercession. Jesus before me, Jesus behind me, Jesus above me, Jesus all around me.

Finish with a Our Father…Hail Mary…Glory Be!

NATIONAL RETREATS/BIBLE STUDIES/SOCIAL MEDIA

Christ Life-Catholic Ministry for Evangelization
https://christlife.org

Malvern Retreat House
https://www.malvernretreat.com

National Shrine of Divine Mercy:
https://www.shrineofdivinemercy.org

Rachel's Vineyard
https://www.rachelsvineyard.org

Women in the New Evangelization
http://catholicvineyard.com

Women of Grace
https://www.womenofgrace.com

Walking with Purpose
https://walkingwithpurpose.com

Instagram Influencers to Follow

Father Robert Baron (bishopbarron)
Crystalina Evert (crystalinaevert)
Pope Francis (franciscus)
Father Rob Galea (frgministry and frrobgalea)
Mark Hart (biblegeek)
Life Teen (Life Teen)
Lila Rose Official (Lila Rose)
Joe Melendrez (joemelendrez)
Father Mike Schmitz (#frmikeschmitz)
Chris Stefanick (Chris Stefanick)
Lysa TerKeurst (lysaterkeurst)

INSTAGRAM CATHOLIC -CHRISTIAN MEDIA ENRICHMENT

Ave Maria Press
Catholic Company
Catholic Answers
Catholic Influencers
The Chosen TV Series
Culture Project
Focus Catholic
FRG Ministry
Gottabesaints
Growing Catholics
Live Action
Living Christian
Relevant Radio
USCCB
The Daily Inspirations
Word on Fire

SMARTPHONE RESOURCES

Bible Verse of the Day
Catholic Daily Readings
CatholicTV
ConfessIt
Catholic Mass Times
Hallow
Laudate
Magnificat

COMPASS CLUB BOOK SHELF

- America Needs Fatima, *The Rosary*. Hanover, PA.: The American Society for the Defense of Tradition, Family and Property, 2020 https://www.americaneedsfatima.org/HP-Accord-Freebies-Desc/free-rosary-guide-booklet.html

- Barbaric, Father Slavic O.F.M., *Fasting*. Dekalb, IL.: Medjugorje Web, 2008 https://www.amazon.com/Fasting-Fr-Slavko-Barbaric-OFM/dp/0972744592

- Bergsma, Dr. John, *Bible Basics for Catholics*. Notre Dame, IN.: Ave Maria Press, 2012 https://www.avemariapress.com/products/bible-basics-for-catholics

- Barber, Terry, *How to Share Your Faith with Anyone A Practical Manual for Catholic Evangelization*. San Francisco, CA.: Ignatius Press, 2018 https://www.ignatius.com/How-to-Share-Your-Faith-with-Anyone-P1109.aspx

- Barron, Father Robert, *The Word on Fire Bible:* The Gospels. Park Ridge, IL.: Word on Fire, 2021 https://www.wordonfire.org/bible/

- Bartunek, Father John, *A Quiet Place: How Daily Prayer Can Change Your Life*. Helena, AL.: Beacon, 2017 https://www.regnumchristi.org/en/quiet-place-fr-john-bartunek-lc/

- Conroy, Susan, *Praying with Mother Teresa*. Stockbridge, MA.: Marian Press, 2016 https://shopmercy.org/praying-with-mother-teresa.html

- Christmyer, Sarah, *Becoming Women of the Word*. Notre Dame, IN.: Ave Maria Press, 2019 https://www.avemariapress.com/products/Becoming-Women-of-the-Word

- Bartunek, Father John LLC PhD, *The Better Part*. Helena, AL.: The Avila Institute, 2013 https://www.sophiainstitute.com/products/item/better-part-4-vol-set

- DeStefano, Anthony, *A Travel Guide to Heaven*. New York, NY.: Image, 2003 https://www.christianbook.com/a-travel-guide-to-heaven/anthony-destefano/9780385509893/pd/509898

- Fireside Catholic Youth Bible. Wichita, KS.: Devore and Sons, Inc. 2004 https://www.firesidecatholic.com/Churches/FiresideCatholicYouthBibleNEXTProgram/

- Flader, Father John, *Why Go to Confession?* Greenwood Village, OH.: Catholic Truth Society-Augustine Institute, 2010https://www.lighthousecatholicmedia.org/store/title/why-go-to-confession-booklet

- Gaitley, Father Michael MIC, *Consoling the Heart of Jesus*. Stockbridge, MA.: Marian Press, 2010 https://www.shopmercy.org/parish-programs/heart-afire.html

- Gaitley, Father Michael *MIC, 33 Days to Morning Glory*. Stockbridge, MA.: Marian Press, 2011 https://www.shopmercy.org/parish-programs/heart-afire.html

- Gray, Tim, *Praying Scripture for a Change, An Introduction to Lectio Divina*. West Chester, PA.: Ascension Press, 2009 https://ascensionpress.com/products/praying-scripture-for-a-change-an-introduction-to-lectio-divina-1

- Hochschild, Joshua, and Christopher Blum, *A Mind at Peace Reclaiming an Ordered Soul in the Age of Distraction*. Manchester, NH.: Sophia Institute, 2017 https://www.sophiainstitute.com/products/item/a-mind-at-peace

- Kempis, Thomas, *The Imitation of Christ.* San Francisco, CA.: Ignatius Press, 2017 https://www.penguinrandomhouse.com/books/91384/the-imitation-of-christ-by-thomas-a-kempis/

- Koenig-Bricker, Woodeene, *365 Mary.* New York, NY.: HarperCollins Publishers, 1997 https://www.christianbook.com/mary-daily-guide-marys-wisdom-comfort/woodeene-koenig-bricker/9780060647445/pd/47442

- Marian Fathers, *Divine Mercy in My Soul-Diary of Saint Maria Faustina Kowalska.* Stockbridge, MA.: Marian Press, 1979 https://www.divinemercy.org/elements-of-divine-mercy/diary/86-diary-of-st-faustina.html

- Makowicz, Heather J, *Peak Encounters: A Spiritual Field Guide for Adventurous Souls.* Orlando, FL.: Xulon Press, 2021 https://www.amazon.com/Peak-Encounters-Inspirational-Reflections-Connect/dp/1662814399

- Martin, Ralph, *The Fulfillment of All Desire.* Steubenville, OH.: Emmaus Road Publishing, 2006 https://stpaulcenter.com/product/the-fulfillment-of-all-desire/

- Mother Angelica, *Living the Scriptures.* Irondale, AL.: EWTN, 2021 https://www.ewtnreligiouscatalogue.com/living-the-scriptures-w-mother-angelica/p/HV000LS

- Pope Francis I, *Gaudete Et Exsultate On the Call to Holiness in Today's World.* Huntington, IL.: Our Sunday Visitor, 2018 https://www.catholiccompany.com/guatete-et-exsultate-on-call-to-holiness-in-todays-world-i125727/

- Philippe, Father Jacques, *Searching for and Maintaining Peace.* Strongsville, OH.: Society of St. Paul, 2002 https://scepterpublishers.org/products/searching-for-and-maintaining-peace

- Philippe, Father Jacques. *Time for God.* Strongsville, OH.: Society of St. Paul, 2002
  https://spiritualdirection.com/2017/01/18/time-for-god-fr-jacques-philippes-classic-on-mental-prayer

- Rolheiser, Ronald, *Prayer our Deepest Longing.* Cincinnati, OH.: Servant Books, 2013
  https://www.dynamiccatholic.com/prayer-our-deepest-longing/PODL.html

- Scallan, Dorothy, *The Golden Arrow.* Charlotte, NC.: Tan Books, 2012 https://www.sistersofcarmel.com/the-golden-arrow-devotion-to-the-holy-face-of-jesus.php

- Tomeo, Teresa, *God's Bucket List.* New York City, NY.: Crown Publishing Group, 2013
  https://www.goodreads.com/book/show/17345212-god-s-bucket-list

- United States Council of Catholic Bishops, *Catholic Catechism for Adults.* Washington, D.C.: United States Council of Catholic Bishops, 2011
  https://www.usccb.org/beliefs-and-teachings/what-we-believe/catechism/us-catholic-catechism-for-adults

- Weddell, Sherry A, *Forming Intentional Disciples*-The Path to Knowing and Following Jesus. Huntington, IL.: Our Sunday Visitor, 2012
  https://www.osvcatholicbookstore.com/product/forming-intentional-disciples-path-to-know-and-follow-jesus

- West, Christopher, *Theology of the Body for Beginners.* West Chester, PA.: Ascension Press, *2019*
  https://ascensionpress.com/products/theology-of-the-body-for-beginners-revised-edition

- Wahlquist, Kelly, *Created to Relate.* Cincinnati, OH.: Servant Books, 2015
  https://catholicvineyard.com/index.php/product/created-to-relate-bundle/

CHRISTIAN-CATHOLIC GIFTS
Wearing and Sharing your Faith

The Catholic Company
https://www.catholiccompany.com

Katholic Beads & More *(Our Lady of Peace Rosaries)*
https://katholicbeadsandmore.com

Love Leigh Gifts *(Arrow necklaces)*
https://www.loveleighgifts.com

*Powerbeads by Jen
https://powerbeadsbyjen.com

*The Compass Club Signature Collection

Faith inspired jewelry was designed and created in collaboration with the author to support the work of the **Stephen Ministry**, a one-to-one, confidential, Christ-centered counseling and caring parish-based outreach for those going through difficult times in life, periods of crisis and challenging transitions. *Twenty five percent of every purchase* will be donated to support the work of those dedicated to supporting the healing process of those who are wounded, suffering and lacking peace in their lives.

COMPASS CLUB MUSIC PLAYLIST:

- Above All - Michael Smith
- Blessed Be Your Name - Newsboys
- Call It Grace - Unspoken
- Chosen - Sidewalk Prophets
- Even If – Mercy Me
- Good Good Father - Chris Tomlin
- God's Not Dead -Newsboys
- I Can Only Imagine – Mercy Me
- I Lift My Hands - Chris Tomlin
- The God Who Stays - Matthew West
- I Surrender to You - Father Rob Galea
- Jesus - Chris Tomlin
- Just Give Me Jesus - Unspoken
- Lord I Need You - Matt Maher
- Lose My Soul -Toby Mac
- Love God Love People - Danny Hokey
- Miracles - Colton Dixon
- No Matter What - Ryan Stevenson
- Oceans – Hillsong United
- Oh Come to the Altar - Elevation Worship
- Only Jesus - Casting Crowns
- Open the Eyes of My Heart – Audrey Assad
- Open the Eyes of My Heart - Michael W. Smith
- Peace Be Still - Hope Darst
- Prodigal Son - Sidewalk Prophets
- The Blessing - Kari Jobe and Cody Carney
- There is Power - Lincoln Brewster
- This is Amazing Grace – Phil Wickham
- Thy Will – Hillary Scott and Scott Family
- You are More - 10 Avenue North
- You Say - Lauren Daigle
- Your Great Name - Natalie Grant
- Word of God Speak – Mercy Me

FOR SPEAKER ENGAGEMENT OR VIRTUAL PRESENTATION OPPORTUNITIES:

Please Contact:

Jackie O'Connor
Jackie@thecompassclub.org

Interested in buying 10 or more copies?

https://www.thecompassclub.org

484.995.8442

ABOUT THE AUTHOR

Jackie O'Connor spent the first twenty years of her career selling textbooks to educators and soliciting manuscripts to be published at the premier college textbook publishing houses.

For the last ten years, she has worked as an educator-evangelist and marketing strategist for various for-profit and non-profit Catholic and Christian organizations. She loves to work with students during their sacramental preparation and being a Eucharistic minister for the homebound.

She enjoys fundraising, playing golf, Mojo Fitness classes, retreats, and above all, spending quality time with her children, close friends, and her loving husband, Jerry.

The peace she has experienced using the intentional living strategies she shares in this book has been life-changing. Her calling to share this spiritual life guide was divinely inspired for many years. Her passion to give back to others who are spiritually hungry and struggling emotionally has been the driving force for this work.

One-hundred percent of the net proceeds from this book will be donated to the **Stephen Ministry**. Stephen Ministry is a Christ-centered lay apostolate and parish-based ministry that offers peaceful support to those facing a major illness, loss of loved one, divorce, job loss, substance abuse, or any other life challenge.

This is Jackie's first book.

CPSIA information can be obtained
at www.ICGtesting.com
Printed in the USA
BVHW020809151121
621683BV00013B/254